How to Stop Common Core

2nd Edition

Marian Armstrong

&

Dave Armstrong

We admit that we are ideological and believe that there is a culture war between liberals and conservatives in our country. It is our struggle, therefore, to NOT see Common Core in political or ideological terms. Regardless, much of what we see in Common Core is a desire for our government to control the thought of our future generations. We reject that.

However, we have made every attempt to try to present a fair picture of Common Core and the people that are pushing it. We claim no conspiracies or some evil intent. Many good people believe in the benefits of Common Core and we respect that.

Even the best of intentions can be wrong. We believe that if you dig into the forces behind Common Core you cannot help but to reject it. We hope we have presented this in a fair and balanced way. We also hope you share this truth and will help us push back against this failure of American education.

We would like to thank Arlene Roemer da Feltre for her wonderful editing in the early days and our friends, Michael Daley and Drusilla Omri for their support and encouragement.

Dave and Marian Armstrong

How to Stop Common Core 2nd Edition

Published by
Armstrong Publishing and Smarty Pants Books
504 N Main St
Livingston, MT 59047

Print ISBN: 978-0-9911845-0-7
eBook ISBN: 978-0-9911845-1-4

Manufactured in the United States of America

For general information on our other products and services please contact our Customer Care Department (406) 223-0090

CONTENTS

What is New in This Second Edition?

We have an online webpage at http://goo.gl/8TqqaD that provides letter and email templates as well as many of the flyers and forms mentioned in this book. We will constantly be adding new links and videos so visit often.

We have added two new chapters on how to automate the sending of letters and emails to the decision makers of Common Core. A single click can send personalized letters to hundreds or even thousands of people you wish to influence.

These new chapters give you step-by-step guides that will help you to effectively communicate to your local, state and federal representatives. You will learn:

1. Instructions on how to Google the names of your local school board members, county officers, teachers and state representatives. We provide a ready to use Excel spreadsheet to hold that information.

2. How to build a list of names, addresses and email addresses in an Excel spreadsheet. You can use this list to mail merge letters or to broadcast emails in your Microsoft Outlook.

3. How to create a simple, but effective personalized letter in MS Word format that you can mail merge to the many local and not so local Common Core decision makers.

4. How to write and personalize an email. With a Microsoft Outlook and few clicks you can broadcast to everyone on your list.

5. Not everyone has Microsoft Office, so we show you how to blast out emails using Gmail and Google Docs. If you use Gmail, you may want to go this way.

The odd looking web URL underlined above is a shortened version of a longer URL.

For example, this:

http://www.theblaze.com/stories/2013/05/28/everything-i-love-about-teaching-is-extinct-teacher-resigns-in-scathing-youtube-video-targeting-standardized-education/

Becomes this:

http://goo.gl/fQCjPa

These shortened links are much easier for you to accurately type. Note that the URL is case sensitive and must be typed exactly as shown. Case is important.

You will see many of these short links in this book. All lead to wonderful web sources that will help you build your case against the implementation of Common Core.

Preface

Who would argue against a program that claimed the following?

> "The Standards are designed to build upon the most advanced current thinking about preparing all students for success in college and their careers. This will result in moving even the best state standards to the next level. In fact, since this work began, there has been an explicit agreement that no state would lower its standards. The Standards were informed by the best in the country, the highest international standards, and evidence and expertise about educational outcomes. We need college and career ready standards because even in high performing states, students are graduating and passing all the required tests and still require remediation in their postsecondary work." [1]

"The Standards" refer to the Common Core State Standards that are being implemented throughout the United States. Why did five states opt out when the program was first presented and presently lawmakers in sixteen additional states are proposing legislation to block the implementation of Common Core?[2] Why are parents expressing outrage about falling math skills and scores or educational content, and becoming involved in the political process to press their states to back out of Common Core?[3] Why are states signing onto a program that overrides their states' rights to control education?[4] Why are citizens throughout the country shocked by the connection between Common Core Standards, federal funds, and the establishment of a database containing immense quantities of private data on students including political affiliations of the student or parent; religious practices, affiliations, or beliefs; sexual behavior or attitudes?[5]

The following document has been written to provide you with information and answers about the Common Core State Standards. In the chapters that follow, you will find out what it is, who created it, and why many educators and parents are troubled by it. If after reading this information, you decide that Common Core is not the way to raise educational standards and that the risks may far outweigh the benefits, then be assured that there is a way out. You will find in these chapters, action points, contact information, and resources to help you take concrete steps.

Two moms led the fight against Common Core in Indiana and succeeded. In the words of one of them, "We were up against so many powerful groups with so much money. We fought against all odds, tons of money, a slew of paid lobbyists. All we had was the truth, the facts, and a passion to protect the future of our children. Our victory is proof that our American system of government still works."[6]

1

1 - Common Core Standards

They tell us these are only standards, Common Core Standards. We soon learn there will be testing, lots of testing. Actually they like to refer to the testing as assessments. They are better known as "high stakes testing" - testing that will determine many things in the life of your child not to mind a teacher's position and salary, a principal's job, whether your school is a failing school or not. Many, many things will be determined by the results of the tests and to pass the tests, we need curriculum which is coming.

It is a stealthy, federal takeover of the educational system in the United States. We are talking about the same standards, same high stake tests, and same Common Core curriculum for every student across the United States. Most parents have not heard of the Common Core program which their governor and state school superintendent signed them onto in return for applying for Race to the Top funds and a possible federal waiver from meeting standards of No Child Left Behind.

Common Core was developed without the U.S. Constitution and state legislative authority. In this "one-size-fits-all" program, schools across America will be controlled by a 'central authority' with no local input concerning what our children learn. In the end, states, parents, students, teachers, communities, or local schools will have NO input. Federal bureaucrats will control and enforce everything. Individual states can add 15% of materials of their own choosing. However, the student will not be tested on that 15%.

Most states have adopted and begun implementation of Common Core Standards in English, language arts, literacy, and math. It is fully expected that the full curriculum, which will include social studies and science, will be completely implemented by 2014. On a side note, already the name has to be changed because Common Core is getting a bad rap. The new Common Core science will be called The Next Generation Science Standard. There will be an extreme amount of data gathering and endless testing done on your children. It might be a good idea to visit with your principal and ask to see your child's file.

Make no mistake about it, Common Core is nationalized education. It is an untested, federally promoted, unfunded experiment with no empirical evidence to show that the new methods of teaching have ever worked. Whatever the claims, no teacher or school board member was asked to contribute to Common Core Standards, nor was any state legislature involved in its creation. Some educators will tell you they had input. They might have had discussions but the real drafters brag about their creation. Some of them have been trying to implement this system for 20 years. There are documents to prove it. History has shown that state-run, top down information control has always led to disastrous results. You need not look any further than in the USSR, Germany, and Cuba.

Claims that Common Core is a state-led initiative is completely false. A nonprofit group called "Achieve Inc." designed the materials. The standards were rubber-stamped by the National Governors Association and the Council of Chief State School Officers, both non-government agencies (NGO's) in DC. They were subsidized by the Gates Foundation. Bill Gates has boasted of having given over $5 billion to change our educational system in America, to nationalize it. He has partnered with UNESCO, charged by the United Nations to nationalize education. Have you heard of Agenda 21? Agenda 21 is the United Nations plan for the 21st century. Common Core is straight out of Agenda 21.

National Standards are set by the 'System'--U.S. Secretary of Education Arne Duncan and his cronies. The National Assessments measure students and teachers. Teachers' salaries are tied to student performance and test scores. In the end, teachers must teach, WORD FOR WORD, to the test' each day. Why? Because their students must pass the tests. In some schools, this is strictly enforced. If you don't believe this, check with states that are further down the road with implementing Common Core Standards!

When President Obama's administration waved $4.35 billion in Race to the Top (RTTT) funds before cash-starved school systems across the country, our educators and politicians went after the money like there were no strings attached. They were desperate for funds. The money was carved out of the 2009 American Recovery and Reinvestment Act (the "stimulus") meaning it was all borrowed money--borrowed from us, the taxpayers. Receiving the money through the stimulus allowed the Obama administration to bypass Congress and bribe states to come on board with the agenda. President Bush set the ground work for Race to the Top with his program of No Child Left Behind. Democrats and Republicans can share the blame in bringing Common Core about.

States had approximately two months to respond, leaving many states to sign on with standards unseen and unwritten in some cases. This two month review period just happened to coincide with most state legislatures being out of session. The Common Core Standards represent at least $16 billion in new unfunded mandates. If the states did not accept the standards, they were threatened with loss of present funding.

States that failed to adopt the Common Core risked losing funding from Title I, a $14.4-billion program that provides funds for low-income students. Most school districts participate in the Title 1 program and need this money to continue programs already established.

This penalty was announced in a White House press release issued on February 22, 2010. It stated that new policies from the Obama administration would "require all states to adopt and certify that they have college and career ready standards in reading and mathematics, which may include common standards developed by a state-led consortium, as a condition for qualifying for Title I funding."[7]

Ben Boychuk, managing editor of School Reform News, tells us about the "voluntary" nature of the standards in his article, "Don't Let Feds Control Local Education":[8]

> The standards are billed as "voluntary," but that's a joke. The Obama administration has already announced plans to make $14 billion in federal Title I funds and another $15 billion in future Race to the Top grants contingent on states adopting the national standards. In short, the standards would be as "voluntary" as reporting personal income to the IRS, regulating the drinking age or maintaining the speed limit. Just try to opt out and see what happens.
>
> The standards are also supposed to be "flexible," but it's difficult to see how. The draft reading and math requirements include detailed, year-by-year prescriptions for every child, regardless of ability. A student who struggles with reading, writing or arithmetic would have an even tougher time keeping up, as teachers would face mounting pressure to cover all the material in federally sanctioned lesson plans.

It would appear that instead of bringing students to the same level, which is impossible with any program, the gifted get by and those struggling or excelling in different modes are only left further behind.

Montana's superintendent Denise Juneau thought No Child Left Behind was egregious. Initially she said Race to the Top's Common Core would not work for Montana because it was a "one-size-fits-all" approach. With No Child Left Behind, the states still controlled their curriculum but had to administer national tests. With Common Core Standards, the federal government controls standards and eventually tests and curriculum.

An example of how one superintendent came to espouse Common Core can be traced in Superintendent Denise Juneau's explanation of Common Core and opposition to it to senate members: "Common Core is a bipartisan state-led initiative across the country. They are, for the first time, standards that 46 states share. So they are really shared standards that raise the bar in English, language arts, and mathematics."[9]

Rigorous, raising the bar, clear standards, etc., are all empty words with no studies to back them up. Professor Thomas Newkirk of the University of New Hampshire has laid out the problems with Common Core in "Speaking Back to the Common Core." He says:[10]

> The Common Core initiative is a triumph of branding. The standards are portrayed as so consensual, so universally endorsed, so thoroughly researched and vetted, so self-evidently necessary to economic progress, so broadly representative of beliefs in the educational community--that they cease to be even debatable. They are held in common; they penetrate to the core of our educational aspirations, uniting even those who might usually disagree. We can be freed from noisy disagreement, and should get on with the work of reform.

Look at their videos, their ad-copy, all of their brochures. They are obviously well-funded. Key words, or talking points that you will hear again and again are rigorous, college and career ready, less information but more in-depth or teaching students how to think. Professor Newkirk continues:

> But I'm left with the question: Who watches the watcher? Who assesses the assessor? That's our job. We've come too far, learned too much, invented too much to diminish our practice by one iota to accommodate the Common Core. When and if we see it impeding our best work, it is not too late to speak up.
>
> In a democracy it is never too late to speak back, to question, to criticize. As Martin Luther King Jr., argued in his "Letter from a Birmingham Jail" it is never "untimely." We simply cannot give up our democratic birthright and settle into compliance, not on something this important. We need to pierce the aura of inevitability that promoters have woven around the Common Core.
>
> We have to "follow the money" and ask who benefits financially from this initiative (especially important considering the financial scandals that occurred with Reading First several years ago). We need to ask about the role of unaccountable think tanks, testing agencies, and foundations in driving this initiative. Have we outsourced reform?
>
> We have to determine what value to place on local control and teacher decision-making. We have to ask about the usefulness of the "data" that tests provide and whether this data may be crowding out the richer, contextual observations of teachers. And we have to look at the limitations of tests themselves, what they can illuminate and what they must ignore. Can they test the complex, integrated, and creative skills that students will truly need--not only to be better workers but more fully realized human beings?

Juneau answered legislators' questions regarding opposition to Common Core. Her reply: "It's a national opposition movement." She proceeded to say that there are a lot of people out there that fear a new way of educating students and because these are such clear standards, a new pathway of learning is required. "There is a lot of movement all across this country opposing Common

Core. I don't really know how to explain it, other than, that it is starting to creep into our state, and people are starting to pick up on that. I know that you've heard a lot from anti-Common Core people. I don't think the fear that is present in the communication you're receiving from those emails and the contacts you're receiving is valid. There is nothing to fear about the Common Core. They are just standards similar to what we've always had."

There are so many fallacies in these statements by Superintendent Denise Juneau that we hardly know where to begin. We trust after reading this book and doing research of your own, you will be able to refute the mistruths that Juneau and other superintendents continue to tell us justifying their decision.

Diane Ravitch, a former assistant U.S. Secretary of Education who was appointed to office by both Clinton and George H.W. Bush, recently changed her mind about Common Core. Ravitch now refutes claims by Obama and Common Core that the standards were created and voluntarily adopted by the states. She writes in The Washington Post, "They were developed by an organization called Achieve and the National Governors Association, both of which were generously funded by the Gates Foundation. There was minimal public engagement in the development of the Common Core. Their creation was neither grassroots nor did it emanate from states."[11]

This page left intentionally blank.

2 - Common Core Curriculum

The curriculum replaces a portion of classics with informational texts and in some cases government documents. According to the American Principles Project, "They de-emphasize the study of classic literature in favor of reading so-called 'informational texts,' such as government documents, court opinions, and technical manuals."[12] Over half the reading materials in grades 6-12 are to consist of informational texts rather than classical literature. This opens the door to future indoctrination.

The Common Core website attempts to assure us that "the Standards require a certain critical content for all students including classic myths and stories from around the world, America's Founding Documents, foundational American literature, and Shakespeare."[13] According to Mary Grabar in Frontpage Magazine the content presented in the sample test reveal that none of the questions came from the "classic myths and stories," etc., cited above.

Many educators believe the study of literary works is essential to a rich, wholesome education. They promote an American cultural identity, pass on Western Judeo-Christian values, inspire independent thought, and develop the imagination. Ms. Grabar believes their elimination is likely to produce citizens incapable of understanding the purpose--and limited--role of the state.

The math standards are equally dismal according to mathematics Professor R. James Milgram of Stanford University. Professor Milgram, the only mathematician on the Validation Committee for Common Core, refused to sign off on the math standards, because they would put many students two years behind those of many high-achieving countries. He explains that Algebra I would be taught in 9th grade, not 8th grade for many students, making calculus inaccessible to them in high school.[14]

Ze'ev Wurman, former U.S. Department of Education official: "Common Core replaces the traditional foundation of Euclidean geometry with an experimental approach. This approach has never been successfully used in any sizable system; in fact, it failed even in the school for gifted and talented students in Moscow, where it was originally invented. Yet Common Core effectively imposes this experimental approach on the entire country, without any piloting."[15]

Rachel Alexander, CP OP-Ed contributor, says the Common Core website uses Orwellian language to deny that the curriculum tells teachers what to teach. The site claims this is a myth: "These standards will establish what students need to learn, but they will not dictate how teachers should teach." [16]Ms. Alexander comments that it is like saying teachers will be required to teach sex education and evolution, but they can choose whether to teach it using assignments, movies, class discussion, or reading."

University of Arkansas professor Sandra Stotsky witnessed Common Core firsthand and concluded: "An English curriculum overloaded with advocacy journalism or with 'informational' articles chosen for their topical and/or political nature should raise serious concerns among parents, school leaders, and policymakers. Common Core's standards not only present a serious threat to state and local education authority, but also put academic quality at risk. Pushing fatally flawed education standards into America's schools are not the way to improve education for America's students."[17]

Michelle Malkin, political commentator and author says, "Bipartisan Common Core defenders claim their standards are merely 'recommendations.' But the standards, 'rubrics' and 'exemplars' are tied to tests and textbooks. The textbooks and tests are tied to money and power. Federally funded and federally championed nationalized standards lead inexorably to de facto mandates. Any way you slice it, dice it or word-cloud it, Common Core is a mandate for mediocrity."[18]

The curriculum accompanying Common Core Standards is a continuum of what has been being taught in our schools for years, for the most part. There are things you need to know about what is being taught to our children.

Danette Clark, journalist, in an article entitled, "Montana Uses Indoctrination Teaching Strategies and Adopts a Radical Resource Recently Banned from Arizona Schools," alerts us to the fact that under the watch of Superintendent Denise Juneau, students in Montana schools and schools across the states are being taught that Christopher Columbus was an invader, thief, and murderer who sailed the world, not to prove that it was round or to share the good news of Jesus (as Columbus wrote), but "to secure the tremendous profits that were to be made by reaching the Indies."[19]

She proceeds to disclose that the Montana Office of Publication uses Rethinking Schools' Rethinking Columbus as a resource for instruction in teaching social studies in Montana. This is the same book that was banned from Arizona schools last year. Check to see if this series is being taught in your schools. Demand that they be banned.

In this particular 'model lesson plan' on Rethinking Columbus, author Bill Beigelow admits he wants to "tell students that they shouldn't necessarily trust the 'authorities,'" and that he sees "teaching as a political action, to equip students to build a truly democratic society."

According to Ms. Clark, the model lesson goes on to give an example of how to engage students through role play. The example explains how the educator tells students that taking Indians as slaves didn't prove profitable enough for Columbus so he sailed to the New World a second time in search of gold and forced the Indians to find it for him. Beigelow (the educator), playing the role of the Indians, pleads with the students (playing Columbus) to release them from slavery. Then Beigelow reads passages from Hans Koning's 'history' book which says that Columbus and his men killed or chopped the hands off of every Native American that was unable to find gold for them.

Many schools rely heavily on techniques of Grant Wiggins and Jay McTighe, both of whom are curriculum developers behind CSCOPE and Common Core. An example of an educational question proposed by Wiggins and McTighe is 'Was George Washington any different from Palestinian terrorists?" Look up Grant Wiggins and Jay McTighe and discover their role in Common Core.[20]

Professor Newkirk raises the question, since the Common Core Standards virtually ignore poetry, will we cease to speak about it? What about character education, service learning? What about fiction writing in the upper high school grades? What about the arts not amenable to standardized testing? What about collaborative learning, an obvious 21st century skill? He says we lose opportunities when we cease to discuss these issues, and allow the Common Core State Standards (CCSS) to completely set the agenda, when the only map is the one it creates.[21]

Always look behind every organization. Who are their chief officers and who is funding them? And then, who in your state is consulting with them? These people need to be questioned and held accountable.

This page left intentionally blank.

3 - Data Tracking

The national Common Core student database was funded with Obama stimulus money and grants from the liberal Bill and Melinda Gates Foundation which largely underwrote and promoted the top-down Common Core Standards program. A division of the conservative Rupert Murdoch's News Corp. built the database infrastructure according to Michelle Malkin.[22] A nonprofit startup, inBloom, Inc., evolved out of this partnership to operate the invasive database, which is compiling everything from health-care histories, income information, and religious affiliations, to voting status, blood types, and homework completion. Both stand to make millions in the technology needed to implement and maintain Common Core.

Joy Pullmann at the Heartland Institute points to a February Department of Education report on its data-mining plans that contemplate the use of student-monitoring techniques such as "functional magnetic resonance imaging" and "using cameras to judge facial expressions, an electronic seat that judges posture, a pressure-sensitive computer mouse and a biometric wrap on kids' wrists." It sounds like science fiction, doesn't it? Go to the Department of Education's very own materials and find out for yourself.

The Department of Education report gives us insight as to what is really behind this new program. It has little to do with raising academic standards and much to do with gathering information on our children. The report reveals Common Core's progressive designs to measure and track children's "competencies" in "recognizing bias in sources," flexibility," "cultural awareness and competence," "appreciation for diversity," "empathy," "perspective taking, trust, and service orientation."[23]

In other words, school districts and state governments are collecting personal data on children's feelings, beliefs, "biases," and "flexibility" instead of imparting knowledge.

The website Truth in American Education says there will be a massive data tracking system on each child with over 400 points of information collected. This information can be shared among organizations and companies, and parents don't have to be informed about what data is being collected. Your child will be watched from preschool till college (P20 Longitudinal Data System). You, the parent, are UNABLE to opt your child out of this tracking.[24]

Local education officials retain legal control over their students' information. But federal law allows them to share files in their portion of the database with private companies selling educational products and services. This is all done in the name of their ability to help each individual student progress in their educational journey.

Gretchen Logue of Missouri Education Watchdog compares this data tracking system to a car navigation system. The learning management systems of the future will know the current location of each learner and be able to plot multiple, individualized paths to the Common Core and other academic goals. She asks the reader, how do you feel about multiple agencies and private organizations tracking your child's every move and data points? If you believe your child is a piece of inventory and human capital, this is a suitable and desirable tracking mechanism.[25]

Every state has a federally funded, interoperable State Longitudinal Database System (SLDS). Every state has accepted 100% federally funded data collection (SLDS). The Data Quality Campaign states: "Every governor and chief state school officer has agreed to build statewide longitudinal data systems that can follow individual students from early childhood through K-12 and postsecondary and into the workforce as a condition for receiving State Fiscal Stabilization Funds as part of the American Recovery and Reinvestment Act (ARRA). A condition of getting the funding (ARRA money) was that the system would be interoperable."[26]

Is the collected private student data accessible to agencies beyond your state education agency? YES, according to Californians Against Common Core, there are state data agencies that connect agencies. The Data Quality Campaign says: "States must ensure that as they build and enhance state K-12 longitudinal data systems, they also continue building linkages to exchange and use information across early childhood, postsecondary and the workforce (P20 workforce) and with other critical agencies, such as health, social services and criminal justice systems."

The Federal Register of December 2011 contains guidelines which state that it is not necessary for a school to get student or parental consent any longer before sharing personally identifiable information. Some say names are expunged but others say there is still an identifiable tag. These guidelines give free range to data collecting leaving parent consent rights a thing of the past. The new recommendations increase the number of potential agencies that have access to private student data. In a nutshell, there is no privacy regulation governing schools anymore. This is illegal under the 10th Amendment.

The Truth in American Education website provides us with an article entitled "Federal Government to have Access to your child's Data via Common Core Assessments".[27] This article gives us insight on how technically state officials can deny that Common Core requires the state to share student data with the federal government.

First, the CCSS are a set of standards identifying what students are expected to learn. The standards themselves do not require any data to be shared with anybody. If that is the case, why do some people claim the Common Core State Standards require states to share student data with the federal government?

The Race to the Top (RTTT) Assessment Program awarded grants to PARCC and SBAC to develop assessments aligned to the CCSS. They each have an identical cooperative agreement. For PARCC, it is called the Cooperative Agreement Between the U.S. Department of Education and the Partnership for Assessment of Readiness of College and Careers. For SBAC, it is called the Cooperative Agreement Between the U.S. Department of Education and the Smarter Balanced Assessment Consortium and the State of Washington (fiscal agent). You can download the Cooperative Agreements from the Race to the Top Assessment Program Awards page. Consortia member states are bound by the terms of these agreements. Are there terms in these agreements parents should be concerned about? YES!

Let's look at the terms that may concern parents having to do with data. You are encouraged to check the cooperative agreement documents for yourself to verify these terms are actually n the agreements. It is established early in the document that ED stands for U.S. Department of Education. Grantee refers to the grant recipient—either PARCC of SBAC. Item 5 on page 3 says:

5) Comply with, and where applicable coordinate with the ED staff to fulfill, the program requirements established in the RTTA Notice Inviting Applications and the conditions on the grant award, as well as to this agreement, including, but not limited to working with the Department to develop a strategy to make student-level data that results from the assessment system available on an ongoing basis for research, including for prospective linking, validity, and program improvement studies; subject to applicable privacy laws.

This establishes that the agreement is referring to student-level (individual) data when it mentions data. The document says nothing about aggregate data.

Item 5(b) on page 11 reads:

(b) Producing all student-level data in a manner consistent with an industry-recognized open-licensed interoperability standard that is approved by the Department during the grant period;

Item 6 on page 10 reads:

6) The Grantee must provide timely and complete access to any and all data collected at

the State level to ED or its designated program monitors, technical assistance providers, or researcher partners, and to GAO, and the auditors conducting the audit required by 34 CFR section 80.26.

If asked, your state officials may deny the Common Core requires the state to share student data with the federal government. While they may not be lying to you they aren't being entirely honest as a result of semantics. Instead of the state sharing data it is the consortia providing access. The state isn't required to share student-level data through the Common Core. The consortia are required to "provide timely and complete access to any and all data collected at the state level" to the federal government. So even the consortia are able to deny they are sharing student data with the federal government. They aren't sharing in the sense of giving, rather they are providing access so the federal government can reach in and take whatever data they want whenever they want.

This is where people get the idea the Common Core requires the state to share student data with the federal government. It really is the federal government requiring the assessment consortia to provide complete access to student-level data.

How can we get free of this system? Jenni White of Restore Oklahoma Public Education states that the only way to get free of this federal data collection invasion is to put political pressure on our governors to give that ARRA money back.[28]

Are teachers also to be studied along with students? YES. The Common Core of Data (CCD) is another federal program of data collection that studies TEACHERS as well as students. It calls itself "a program of the U.S. Department of Education's National Center for Education Statistics that annually collects fiscal and non-fiscal data about all public schools, public school districts, and state education agencies in the United States. The data are supplied by state education officials and include information that describes schools and school districts, including name, address, and phone numbers; descriptive information about students and staff, including demographics; and fiscal data, including revenues and current expenditures." The system also allows the governments to track, steer and even to punish teachers, students and citizens more easily."[29]

How does Common Core relate to the federal and corporate data collection movement that we are witnessing in the nightly news? Chief of Staff Joanne Weiss at the Department of Education has been publicly quoted as saying that "data-mashing" is a good idea. Secretary of Education Arne Duncan gives speeches calling for "more robust data." At a recent White House Datapalooza, it was stated that Common Core tests were the glue for open data. Without them, this data movement would be impossible.[30] Think about that. It is the tests that make the data collection possible! Is this whole movement about raising standards or is it as Rosa Koire says all about "inventory and control?"

4 - National Testing

High stakes testing has been tried for years and rarely do you find anyone in the educational system endorsing them or seeing any positive effects they have on improving education and true learning. Teachers hate them, students hate them, and parents hate them. Study after study has been done showing only increased stress on all involved being accomplished.

Yet, our experts from DC are pushing them down our schools' throats with no end to testing. Through Common Core and other similar programs, standardized testing has come to dominate our schools and severely compromise teachers' ability to do their jobs. Having to push countless practice prep tests takes too much time away from true learning.

We can't say enough about how detrimental standardized tests are to our children. They provide only one indicator of student achievement. Teachers are tempted to teach to the test, which narrows the curriculum and encourages cheating. We must demand that standardized tests not be used in high stakes decisions affecting students, teachers, and schools.

In her article "Parents fight against high stakes tests and the common core,"[31] journalist Kristen Layelle reports that where teachers were once able to inspire and motivate students to become passionate, creative thinkers, teachers are now forced to teach scripted, mind-numbing (literally), and fast- paced Common Core material, which leaves no room for the teachers to teach to the individual student.

Layelle says, "I have spoken to teachers who are literally in tears when talking about what state tests have done to their teaching styles. They now feel like drones, force feeding the kids' hours upon hours of test prep work."

Do these tests have any educational value or are they simply used to evaluate teachers, principals and schools?

Over 15,000 New Yorkers sent the following petition to Governor Cuomo and the legislature to end high stakes testing in New York:[32]

We believe the following:

- High stakes testing lowers the quality of education due to "teaching to the test." It reduces time for the enrichment students need and enjoy, while increasing unhealthy emotional stress in our children.
- Testing results belong to students and families. They should not be used to close schools, retain students or evaluate educators, and they should never be used for commercial purposes nor given to national databases.
- Schools should be safe havens where students feel secure and cared for, not sorted and ranked by test scores. They should not be places where children feel inadequate, stressed and unsuccessful. No nine-year-old should be told whether he is in a road to "college readiness." It is absurd to try to make such predictions.
- All tests and student results should be available to teachers and parents after test administration. They should be used only to inform parents and teachers about a child's learning and to improve instruction. Tests should exist to serve students, not politicians or for-profit testing companies. Testing exists to serve our students. Our students do not exist to serve testing.

A coalition of more than 130 Massachusetts professors and researchers from some 20 schools--including Harvard, Tufts, Boston and Brandeis Universities--signed a new public statement that urges officials to stop overusing high stakes standardized test to assess students, teachers and schools.[33]

Their statement is the latest effort in a revolt against high stakes testing that has spread from coast to coast. Students are opting out of taking standardized tests, teachers are refusing to administer them and some superintendents are criticizing the standardized test-based accountability systems passed in various states.

A study done by two Arizona State University Professors (Amrien and Berliner) came to a number of conclusions about high stakes testing. They studied 16 states that had implemented high stakes high school graduation exams. Their paper was entitled "An Analysis of Some Unintended Consequences of High Stakes Testing."[34]

Their results showed higher numbers of low-performing students being retained in grade before pivotal testing years, higher numbers of low- performing students being suspended before testing days, students expelled from school before tests, or reclassified as exempt from testing because they are determined to be either Special Education or Limited English Proficient -all strategies to prevent low-scoring students from taking high stakes testing.

Their study also showed that higher numbers of students are being prevented from opportunities to learn subjects such as art, music, science, social studies, and physical education. Because these subjects are not often tested, teachers and administrators tend to focus less on them. The study showed that higher numbers of urban school teachers, in particular, are "teaching to the test," limiting instruction to only those things that are sure to be tested thus requiring students to spend hours memorizing facts. And instances of cheating by teachers and other school personnel can easily be a response to the pressures of high stakes testing.

On the website *Education Week Teacher*, Anthony Cody published the article "Time for Teacher Unions to Hop Off the Common Core Train."[35] He has this to say about high stakes testing:

> Many teachers have been in a honeymoon phase with the Common Core, before the inevitable high stakes tests arrive. It is understandable that teachers who have suffered under the lash of NCLB (No Child Left Behind) would view a new system with some hope. However, that honeymoon is coming to an end, as the high stakes tests arrive, and we discover them to be more pervasive, invasive and expensive than the ones they are replacing. And when the results come, and show our students scoring significantly lower, we will awaken to a fresh indictment of our supposedly broken schools.
>
> The Common Core is a Trojan horse for a whole set of curriculum and instructional tools--hardware as well as software, that will require a massive initial investment, and significant ongoing expenses in terms of maintenance, new subscriptions and software, and replacement of computers every few years. Vendors and "innovators" are salivating at the chance to carve out a larger share of the education market. We are in something of a zero sum game. They believe that they can "personalize" education by getting each child in front of his own computer screen for half the day. We know there are huge problems with this approach, but that is what is most efficient. And having a national set of standards and assessments means you have a single market for all these "innovations."
>
> Secondly, the tests are already arriving, as we have seen in New York. And they are terrible. We were promised a "next generation" of assessments that would be so much smarter. Tests that adjust their difficulty as students respond. These are the very sorts of tests that the teachers and students in Seattle are boycotting. The hours spent on testing is doubling, tripling. We are testing third graders on computers. I spoke with kindergarten teachers last week in California who must spend an hour-and-a-half testing each child in their class three times a year. That turns into three weeks of testing, repeated fall, winter and spring. Nine weeks of teaching lost! As parents become aware of these tests they are up in arms. The opt-out movement is gaining strength rapidly in New York, as the new tests arrive.

This page left intentionally blank.

5 - End Goal of Common Core

On the website American Thinker, Dean Kalahar makes the following charge:[36]

> Common Core is not about standards, it's about gaining control over the education system in a futile attempt to create a Progressive utopia using the important sounding academic umbrella of 'standards.' But ask yourself, haven't educators always had standards, guidelines, or benchmarks to guide curriculum? Please understand this is about power, control, and the agenda! Common Core is just the host carrier of the disease --Progressive Secularism.

Further proof of totalitarian control is seen in Common Core's nationwide tracking system. Michelle Malkin writes that the 2009 stimulus included a "State Fiscal Stabilization Fund" that mandated constructing "longitudinal data systems (LDS) to collect data on public-school students"[37] that resulted in the National Education Data Model. Then in 2012, the U.S. Department of Education rewrote federal privacy laws to let it share a child's academic record with virtually anyone.

Ohioans against Common Core had this to say about the end game in implementing Common Core to all the states across the nation:[38]

> The agenda-driven policy makers have aligned with crony capitalists to exploit the legal monopoly that is government education. Under the guise of "education reform," the social engineers are hard at work violating our children's civil liberties, privacy, and education opportunities. Our children have been reduced to nothing more than "human capital" (their words) to be trained for the benefit of "community stakeholders" (words already in the Ohio Revised Code). Our children will now be defined by the 400 data points that bureaucrats and big business have determined critical to manage their "cradle to career" path and develop a "21st Century workforce."

> Thanks to holes punched in the Family Education Rights & Privacy Act (FERPA), those points will be personally identifiable and shared with not just the federal DOE, HHS & Labor, but with third party "for profits" as well. While the wonders of Common Core rhetoric runneth over, nowhere in the massive design to nationalize education does one read a reference to the inherent value of the individual child or of the established parental authority which supersedes the state. It's all about the collective. It's all about control."

Superintendents, principals, curriculum directors and state educational directors will argue they still have control. Of course, they are giving up local control. You need look no further than to the fact that the Standards are copyrighted. Just a little investigation on their part would lead them to the players behind Common Core and Race to the Top. Maybe they agree that our schools would be better served with the Federal Government nationalizing our education in America. Most Americans do not agree with that and want to keep control over their children's education as both the State and U.S. Constitutions provides for.

In 2009, when Race to the Top money was dangled in front of cash- starved states, Superintendent Juneau said Montana schools were doing well and shouldn't conform to "one-size-fits-all" federal reforms. What happened from the fall of 2009 to the spring of 2010? Common Core didn't change.

Governor Brian Schweitzer, ex-governor of Montana, goes on to explain that perhaps with "state revenues shrinking and school districts facing a grim budget outlook, it appears the chance to apply for $20 million to $75 million in one-time federal money has proven irresistible. How many other governors found themselves in the same place?

Eric Feaver, union leader is quoted as saying, "Montana is in difficulties [sic] in financial resources and it's probably not wise simply to thumb our nose at the federal government and say, 'No way, Jose'. It's one-time money, but we've been funding a lot of things with one-time-only money. When times are really tight, you'll take your revenue streams wherever you can find them. How do you like that for selling our children's education to the top bidder?[39]

There was not only the Race to the Top program where you could get money, but other grants as well with many strings attached, if the state signed on to Common Core. Or, did their decision have something to do with President Obama threatening to withhold Title I funds to states that did not jump on board with his program? Or did it have something to do with the fact that over half of Montana's schools would be announced as "failed schools" under the No Child Left Behind program and if you signed on to Race to the Top, you might get a waiver from the NCLB?

6 - Legality of Common Core

Currently, the United States does not have a national school curriculum. However, that would change with Common Core being implemented nationwide. In accordance with the 10th Amendment of the U.S. Constitution, the ultimate authority to create and administer education rests with the states.

The American Recovery and Reinvestment Act of 2009 ("stimulus") had no provisions for use of the funds but Secretary of Education Arne Duncan created a program, Race to the Top, which violated U.S. laws stating that the Federal government is not to influence state and local education policies.

The Common Core Standards/Race to the Top never came before Congress for public hearings, debate, and a floor vote; and that is the reason the Obama administration has been able to capture the public schools of the country without the public's knowledge. The federal government is forbidden by public law to take over state and local school education systems. The federal government is forbidden by public law to meddle in curriculum and programs of instruction used at the local school level. Common Core Standards and Race to the Top violates all of the above.

Lindsey M. Burke, an education policy analyst from The Heritage Foundation, issued a report posing legal questions regarding Common Core.[40] She brings to our attention a new report by former U.S. Education Department officials questioning the legality of federal support for the Common Core State Standards Initiative, a set of education standards which critics say will lead to a national curriculum and tests.

The organizations developing the Core and related tests are funded by the Department of Education. This consortium is also "'helping' states move to national standards and assessments, as well as developing 'curriculum frameworks' and 'instructional modules,'" Jim Stergios from Pioneer Institute said.[41]

These actions, the authors argue, break three laws that prohibit federal involvement in curriculum: the General Education Provisions Act, the Department of Education Organization Act, and the Elementary and Secondary Education Act.

"I hate to be so blunt, but the U.S. Department of Education is violating three federal laws," Jim Stergios said. "And the fact is that state and local officials who are part of the national standards and assessment efforts are compliant in the breaking of these federal laws."

The report "The Road to a National Curriculum" concludes that the Obama administration "has simply paid others to do that which it is forbidden to do."

"The concern is that the assessments developed by the two Race to the Top-funded consortia will end up illegally directing the course of elementary and secondary curriculum across the nation," said report coauthor Kent Talbert.

The report from the Pioneer Institute for Public Policy Research carries weight because of its authors. Talbert is the former general counsel for the U.S. Department of Education (DOE) and chief legal advisor to former Education Secretary Margaret Spellings, and Bob Eitel is a former deputy general counsel for the agency. Bill Evers, former U.S. Assistant Secretary of Education and now a Hoover Institution scholar also contributed.

"The paper establishes how, through the Race to the Top fund, the RTTT Assessment Program, and federal waivers of No Child Left Behind, the USDOE is pushing states to adopt standards and assessments that are favored by the Department," said Pioneer Institute.

In this same article Ms. Burke reports that Arne Duncan "floats 'Bizarre' No Child Waivers for School Districts." Forty-six states have adopted the Common Core. The Obama administration required applicants for Race to the Top grants and for waivers of No Child Left Behind's most punitive provisions to adopt the standards. The report alleges tying these strings to federal favors shows significant involvement in implementing the Core nationwide.

7 - Cost of Common Core

No one apparently knows the cost of Common Core. Actually no one could know the cost. It is a total unknown. Estimates are high though. It is a question we need to keep asking. Start locally and find out from your local school board trustees, city manager, county commissioners and city commissioners. They can tell us what the projected educational cost for our particular county is for the next school years.

The Pioneer Institute published an in-depth financial analysis of Common Core. They identify three key areas of projected new costs: assessment, professional development, and textbooks and instructional materials with substantial new expenditures for technology infrastructure support.[42]

- Over a typical standards time horizon of seven (7) years, we project Common Core implementation costs will total approximately $15.8 billion across participating states. This constitutes a "mid-range" estimate that only addresses the basic expenditures required for implementation of the new standards. It does not include the cost of additional expensive or controversial reforms that are sometimes recommended to help students meet high standards, such as performance-based compensation or reduced class sizes.

- Total, seven-year costs include the following additional expenses: $1.2 billion for the new assessments, $5.3 billion for professional development, $2.5 billion for textbooks and instructional materials, and $6.9 billion for technology infrastructure and support.

- $10.5 billion of the projected amount is for "one-time" costs that include familiarizing educators with the new standards, obtaining aligned textbooks and instructional materials, and sufficiently enhancing technology infrastructure to implement the Common Core online assessments for all students.

Here are what some other counties are finding out about the cost of Common Core. School officials in some Long Island counties are reporting that the money in grants won't come close to covering the cost of buying new texts, hiring outside agencies to grade exams, training teachers and administrators, and paying for substitutes to work in their place, among other expenses required by the program.

The Rockville Centre school board on Long Island voted recently to turn down the district's $34,230 Race to the Top award. Chris Pellettieri, assistant superintendent for curriculum and instruction, said the district would have to invest $150,000 in testing, scoring, training and other payments.[43]

Jane Modoono, a New York high school principal, said her district was to get $28,000 and pulled out early. "We figured it would cost us between $100,000 and $200,000 per year," she said. "It was money we could spend in a much better way than this."

In Eagle Forum's Educator Reporter, an article entitled "Common Core Standards Aren't Cheap" reports:[44]

> As states look for ways to relieve the pressure brought on by ever-shrinking education budgets, it is to be hoped that they will reconsider the monumental financial cost of their hasty commitment to Common Core Standards. On December 1, the Education Task Force of the American Legislative Exchange Council (ALEC) took the first step toward passing model legislation to provide states with a Common Core exit strategy. A number of states may soon introduce the legislation, which relies on Closing the Door on Innovation, a document endorsed by 350 prominent teachers, parents, education policymakers, and researchers. Closing the Door on Innovation argues that:
>
> 
>
> 1. There is no constitutional or statutory basis for national standards, national assessments, or national curricula.
>
> 
>
> 2. There is no consistent evidence that a national curriculum leads to high academic achievement.
>
> 3. The national standards on which the administration is planning to base a national curriculum are inadequate.
>
> 4. There is no body of evidence for a "best" design for curriculum sequences in any subject. There is no evidence to justify a single high school curriculum for all students.

The Heritage Foundation's Lindsay Burke has also suggested an exit strategy:[45]

> First, states ought to find out which body agreed to adopt the Common Core Standards.

Usually the state board of education is at fault — a fact that ought to concern citizens, since Common Core represents an abdication of the school board's constitutionally-mandated responsibilities.

Next, states ought to outlaw new spending for standards implementation until independent cost analyses are performed and taxpayers notified about the new expenditures. Third, state leaders ought to work to determine how each individual state can best restore standards and curriculum control to its own local governing bodies. Many current state officials were elected after the standards were adopted in 2010. These newly elected leaders need to be aware of the changes the Common Core Standards would entail, and they need to strengthen existing state standards and tests.

It was your current Superintendent of Education and governor who are largely responsible for signing onto Common Core. They need to hear from you weekly! After reading this book, it is hoped that you will have many questions to ask them.

This page left intentionally blank.

8 - Players Behind Common Core

In their article "Who Is Behind Common Core?" Arizonians Against Common Core make the following claims:[46]

> A nonprofit organization called Achieve, Inc., in Washington, D.C. is the main driving force behind creating the Common Core State Standards Initiative (CCSSI). The Common Core (CC) standards were initiated by private interests in Washington, D.C., without any representation from the states.
>
> From the Achieve, Inc. website: "To this day, Achieve remains the only education reform organization led by a Board of Directors of governors and business leaders. This unique perspective has enabled Achieve to set a bold and visionary agenda over the past 15 years, leading Education Week in 2006 to rank Achieve as one of the most influential education policy organizations in the nation."
>
> Eventually the creators of the Common Core State Standards Initiative (CCSSI) realized the need to present a facade of state involvement, and therefore, enlisted the National Governors Association (NGA) {a trade association that doesn't include all governors}, and the Council of Chief State School Officers (CCSSO) another DC-based trade association. Neither of these groups have grant authority from any particular state or states to write the standards.

Achieve, Inc., a DC-based nonprofit, includes many progressive education reformers who have been advocating national standards and curriculum for decades. Massive funding for all this came from private interests such as The Bill and Melinda Gates Foundation.

As with all public/private partnerships, the real winners are revealed along the money trail. In the case of Common Core Standards, the winners are the centralized control educrats, the U.S.

Department of Education, big business including Bill Gates (Microsoft), Pearson Publishing and of course the campaign coffers of politicians from BOTH parties.

In her article "Hogwash Alert to National Review Online" Christel Swasey in a thorough, well documented study exposes the Common Core Standards and those pushing it. Swasey reports that "Gates is the biggest promoter and funder of Common Core. His money is behind almost everyone who supports Common Core. Bill Gates has said he's spent $5 billion pushing (his version) of education reform."[47] Swasey continues:

> He's bribed the national PTA to advocate for Common Core to parents; he's paid the CCSSO to develop Common Core; and he owns opinion maker Education Week magazine. There's a near-endless list of Gates' attempts (very successful, I might add) to foist his vision of education without voter input.
>
> In 2004, Gates signed a 26 page agreement with UNESCO to develop a master curriculum for global teacher training. Robert Muller, the former assistant secretary general of the U.N. is the grandfather of the world core curriculum, the goal being to bring all schools in all nations under one Common Core Curriculum.
>
> Republican Jeb Bush is behind the Foundation for Excellence in Education, a nongovernmental group which pushes Common Core and is, of course, funded by Gates. Republican Rupert Murdoch owns not only Fox News, but also the Common Core implementation company Wireless Generation that's creating Common Core testing technology. Democrat Bob Corcoran, President of GE Foundation (author of cap and trade and carbon footprint taxes to profit GE on green tech) and 49% owner of NBC also bribed the PTA to promote Common Core, and gave an additional $18 million to the states to push Common Core implementation. Corcoran was seen recently hobnobbing with Utah's Republican Lt. Governor Greg Bell, business leaders in the Chamber of Commerce, and has testified in the education committee that the opponents of Common Core in Utah "are liars".
>
> This battle is between the collusion of corporate greed and political muscle versus the individual voter. It's a battle between the individual student, teacher, or parent versus huge public-private partnerships. That's the David and Goliath here.
>
> The Common Core movement is not about what's best for children. It's about greed and political control. A simple test: if Common Core was about helping students achieve legitimate classical education, wouldn't the Common Core experiment have been based on empirical study and solid educator backing?
>
> Where's the basis for what proponents call "rigorous," "internationally competitive," and "research-based"? Why won't the proponents point to proof of "increased rigor" the way the opponents point to proof of increased dumbing down?

Many educators are crying out--even testifying to legislatures--that Common Core is an academic disaster. I'm thinking of Professors Christopher Tienken, Sandra Stotsky, Thomas Newkirk, Ze'ev Wurman, James Milgram, William Mathis, Susan Ohanian, Charlotte Iserbyt, Alan Manning, and others.

Let's look at the Common Core textbooks. Virtually every textbook company in America is aligning now with Common Core. (So even the states that rejected Common Core, and even private schools and home schools are in trouble; how will they find new textbooks that reflect Massachusetts' high standards?)

Pearson's latest textbooks show extreme environmentalism and a global-citizen-creating agenda that marginalizes national constitutions and individual rights in favor of global collectivism. The biggest education sales company of all the Common Core textbook and technology sales monsters on the planet is Pearson, which is led by mad "Deliverology" globalist Sir Michael Barber. Watch his speeches.

He doesn't just lead Pearson, the company that is so huge it's becoming an anti-trust issue. Sir Michael Barber also speaks glowingly of public-private partnerships, of political "revolution," "global citizenship" and a need for having global data collection and one set of educational standards for the entire planet. He's a political machine. Under his global Common Core, diversity, freedom and local control of education need not apply.

Along with some of the gold-rushing colluders chasing Common Core-alignment product sales, there are political individuals calling educational shots, and these are without exception on the far, far left. And of these, the National Review is correct in saying that their goal to nationalize U.S. Education has been happening since long before Obama came to power.

But they are wrong in saying that Common Core isn't a road map to indoctrinating students into far left philosophy. Power players like Linda Darling-Hammond and Congressman Chakra Fattah ram socialism and redistribution down America's throat in education policy, while Pearson pushes it in the curriculum.

It's safe to say that Linda Darling-Hammond has as much say as anyone in this country when it comes to education policy. She focuses on "equity" and "social justice"; that is, redistribution of wealth using schools. Reread that last sentence.

Darling-Hammond has worked for CCSSO (Common Core developer) since long before the standards were even written. She served on the standards validation committee. She now works for SBAC (the Common Core test writer); she also consults with AIR (Utah's Common Core test producer) and advises Obama's administration; she promotes the secretive CSCOPE curriculum and more.

So yes, there is an undeniable socialism push in Common Core textbooks and in the Department of Education.

The article insists that Common Core is not a curriculum; it's up to school districts to choose curricula that comply with the standards. Sure. But as previously noted: 1) all the big textbook companies have aligned to Common Core. Where are the options? 2) Common Core tests and the new accountability measures threaten teachers with losing their jobs. This insures teachers will only teach Common Core standards.

The article claims that states who have adopted Common Core could opt out, "and they shouldn't lose a dime if they do", but Title I monies have been threatened, and the No Child Left Behind waiver is temporary on conditions of following Common Core. Those states that did get Race to the Top money would have to return it.

Besides Achieve, Inc.; CCSSO; the Obama administration; and Rupert Murdoch; Karen Bracken, who presented an overview of Common Core to the Tennessee Tea Party, claims the following individuals to be key players behind Common Core:[48]

- George Soros
- Pearson Foundation--UK publishing company--Sir Michael Barber (Globalist/works for Pearson)
- Bill Ayers and his good friend Linda Darling-Hammond (far left radicals).
- Jeb Bush--Foundation for Excellence in Education (FEE) and "Chiefs for Change"
- Marc Tucker--long-time associate of Bill and Hillary Clinton; educational radical
- David Coleman--His Student Achievement Partners played a leading role in developing Common Core Standards for math and literacy. He now sits as the head of the College Examination Board which received $30M from Gates. Coleman said he will align the SAT with Common Core. ACT is already aligned. "What children need," asserts Coleman, "is a close reading of 'informational text.' No creation of new worlds. The teacher's job is to make sure kids stick just to the text." Informational text, pronounces Coleman, is what will give students the world knowledge necessary to compete as workers in the Global Economy...Coleman insists that teachers must train students to be workers in the global economy.
- UNESCO - United Nations Education, Scientific and Cultural Organization
- The Big Three: Bill and Melinda Gates Foundation--major funding for just about every facet involved in Common Core; Walton Family Foundation; Eli & Edythe

Broad Foundation.

Going deeper..................Marc Tucker

Nov. 11, 1992 Marc Tucker (President - National Center on Education and the Economy NCEE) sends the infamous "Dear Hillary" letter. The 18 page letter lays out a plan "to remold the entire American system" into "a seamless web that literally extends from cradle to grave and is the same system for everyone," coordinated by "a system of labor market boards at the local, state and federal levels" where curriculum and "job matching" will be handled by counselors" accessing the integrated computer-based program.

Tucker's ambitious plan was implemented in three laws passed by Congress and signed by President Clinton in 1994: the Goals 2000 Act, the School-to-Work Act, and the reauthorized Elementary and Secondary Education Act. These laws establish the following mechanisms to restructure the public schools:

1. Bypass all elected officials on school boards and in state legislatures by making federal funds flow to the Governor and his appointees on workforce development boards.

2. Use a computer database, a.k.a. "a labor market information system," into which school personnel would scan all information about every schoolchild and his family, psychological, behavioral, and interrogations by counselors. The computerized data would be available to the school, the government, and future employers.

3. Use "national standards" and "national testing" to cement national control of tests, assessments, school honor and rewards, financial aid, and the Certificate of Initial Mastery (CIM), which is designed to replace the high school diploma.

   - UNESCO (United Nations Education, Scientific and Cultural Organization)

   - December 31, 1984 Reagan withdraws the US from UNESCO due to anti-western, far-left propaganda

   - 2003 George Bush reunites the US and UNESCO

Washington Times, January 18, 2004 "Learning Globally"

The Bush administration has begun issuing grants to spread a United Nations sponsored school program that aims to become a "universal curriculum" for teaching global citizenship called IB

George Walker, IB's .director-general in Geneva, said in June "the program remains committed to changing children's values so they think globally, rather than in parochial national terms from their own country's viewpoint...."

The IB curriculum, UNESCO said, would promote human rights and social justice; the need for "sustainable development" (Agenda 21); and address population, health, environmental and immigration concerns.

In one of its first efforts in 1949, the UNESCO textbook titled "Toward World Understanding," used to teach teachers what to teach, said: "As long as the child breathes the poisoned air of nationalism, education in the world-mindedness can produce only rather precarious results. As we have pointed out, it is frequently the family that infects the child with extreme nationalism."

The prime mover for UNESCO back in 1945 was Julian Huxley. Huxley served as its first Director. Huxley also served as the VP of Eugenics Society from 1937-1944. In 1947 Huxley wrote: "Thus even though it is quite true that any radical eugenic policy will be for many years politically and psychologically impossible, it will be important for UNESCO to see that the eugenic problem is examined with the greatest of care, and that the public mind is informed of the issues at stake so that much that now is unthinkable may at least become thinkable.

Bill Gates

In Paris on November 17, 2004 Bill Gates signed a "Cooperation Agreement" with UNESCO. On signing every page of this agreement Bill Gates/Microsoft agrees to support the objectives of the UNESCO Constitution. And to advance Millennium Development Goals for Universal Basic Education, Master Syllabus for Teacher Training, UNESCO is responsible for content development.

Bill and Melinda Gates Foundation is a major funder of Common Core. They have spent approximately $173 million to bribe anyone that gets in the way and form partnerships that give him total control. National PTA, Achieve, NGA, CCSSO, NCEE, is just the short list.

2011 Gates and Pearson Foundation join a partnership to offer on line courses/eBooks.

Bill and Melinda Gates Foundation and the British Government co-host a new London conference on eugenics with global coalition partners such as American Planned Parenthood (founder Margaret Sanger - eugenicist), British Marie Stopes international (Marie Stopes - eugenicist), and the United Nations Populations Fund. Bill Gates father was a member of national board of Planned Parenthood.

Bill Gates is also heavily invested in Monsanto (500,000 * Millennium Development Goals - A set of 8 goals with the completion objective of 2015. UNESCO supports the Earth Charter.

This page left intentionally blank.

9 - Unions and Common Core

The unions for the most part are backing Common Core which is a bit puzzling in itself. There are unions across the country that are expressing opposition to Common Core, in one case, even taking out ads opposing it. Teacher unions don't want to get rid of it; in fact, they say it's a good idea. But they do want to slow down parts of its implementation.

"The Common Core is in trouble," said Randi Weingarten, current president of the American Federation of Teachers, spoke in New York about the issue. "There is a serious backlash in lots of different ways, on the right and on the left."[49]

Weingarten asked that there be a moratorium on the high stakes decisions attached to the testing that goes along with Common Core. "This is a wake-up call for everyone else in the country," she said, pointing to New York, which just administered new tests based on the Common Core standards. Teachers, parents, and students complained that the tests were poorly designed, covered material that had not been taught, and frustrated children to the point of tears.

New York, like many other states, plans to use the test results in decisions about student grade promotion, teacher job evaluations, and school closings. But Weingarten is calling for a moratorium on consequences for at least one year until teachers and students across the country are sufficiently steeped in the Common Core standards. New York and Kentucky are the only states to have begun testing based on the new standards; the others will follow in 2014.

Lucy Calkins, a professor at Teachers' College at Columbia University, has launched a website where hundreds of teachers, principals and parents have posted feedback--overwhelmingly negative--about the new tests in New York.

"I'm a big supporter of the Common Core. I wrote the best-selling book about it," Calkins said, "But this makes even me question it."[50]

A New York state teachers union has come out against Common Core State standards and has started an online petition. In an online article entitled "Growing Concerns About Common Core Tests" John Pavone of the Rochester Teachers Association Union says “It’s a setup for failure."[51] Teachers are worried they will be evaluated based on a curriculum that they are not fully trained in. Pavone continues, "They’re going to blame me if the kids can’t pass the test and the kids can’t pass the test. It’s set up in such a way that you can’t pass the test.”

“Nobody was prepared for these changes,” Moran (a parent) said. “There was no public discussion about it. The parents weren’t prepared for it. Frankly I don’t think the teachers or administration was prepared for it.”

“It’s going to be a disaster,” said retired Rochester principal Dan Drmacich, a frequent critic of testing. “You’re going to have at least 30 percent statewide failures on this and that’s because they haven’t given teachers time to teach or kids time to learn it.”

Tim Slekar runs the website THE CHALK FACE knows SCHOOLS MATTER. In his article "Union Leaders Love Common Core: Why?"[52] He explores this phenomenon of unions and Common Core:

> How is it possible that AFT leadership endorses mass experimentation on the nation’s public school children? What’s in it for the union leadership? What negotiations took place that convinced union leadership to support inserting a national curriculum with no empirical data to be used in the education of our children?
>
> As a parent, teacher, and researcher I am disgusted. Anyone following the attack on public education knows that adoption of the Common Core will lead to more narrowing of the curriculum, more test prep, more teaching to the test and more teacher bashing when the results of the new test scores are used to judge America’s public school teachers.
>
> Are there any members in the national teachers’ unions willing to challenge the misguided leadership that continues to sell out your professionalism and now supports selling out the education of the children?
>
> Unions are to represent the teachers and Common Core is a nightmare for teachers. Their job and salaries are tied to the performance of the students on tests which forces them to teach to the test. When the standards, curriculum and test are all in place they will become functionaries.

Just a thought--Bill Gates keeps pouring millions into unions--could that have anything to do with why unions are on board with Common Core?

10

10 - Common Core with Private and Home Schools

Bottom line for all students: public, private or home schooled children are, you must past the tests! The SAT, ACT and GED are all being aligned with Common Core. If you want to go to a major university, you must score well on the tests which are used as entrance exams.

From Oklahomans against Common Core:[53]

> Did you know that private schools and charter schools are turning to Common Core so they will have books to use that contain "COMMON" curricula developed for the standards so private school students will have the same advantage as government school kids on tests such as ACT--which are being shaped to match the standards?
>
> Many large textbook companies like Pearson, threw their lot in with the Council of Chief State School Officers (a private national association) and the National Governor's Association (also a private association to which NOT all governors belong) to create and insinuate the CCSS in American government schools. The free market is wonderful, but in this case, textbook companies with smaller market share are forced to mold their materials to the CCSS or lose business to those companies producing CCSS-aligned texts.
>
> This also works with education retailers. Did you know that companies who sell to the home school market, like Mardel, are selling Common Core materials?
>
> Not only that, but what if home school students are forced to test to the Common Core as they are implemented across states? What if universities will no longer take transcripts of home school students if they haven't been taught using the COMMON standards or they haven't taken the CCSS standardized tests? In fact, the Home School Legal Defense Association has condemned the CCSS for these and other reasons.

> In closing, why follow blindly behind School Choice advocates when there is really NO CHOICE in education as long as states are perpetuating the CCSS?
>
> It is important--no necessary--to make sure Republicans pushing these Obama/Duncan overreaching education reforms understand that parents understand the issue of Core vs. Choice. Let's let legislators, the media and School Choice advocates know we will NOT raise COMMON children here in Oklahoma and that Common Core is NOT OK!

Michelle Malkin reports on what is in store for today's two million home schoolers and the hundreds of thousands of American adults taking the GED test annually: "In March 2013, New Readers Press, a publishing division of ProLiteracy--the world's largest organization of adult basic education and literacy programs--released a revised edition of its bestselling Scoreboost series for the 2014 GED test. With eight supplemental workbooks on the mathematics, language arts, science, and social studies tests, the new series is aligned with the Common Core State Standards and has been expanded, according to the publisher, "to cover the complexities of the new math test as well as the analytic writing required by the extended-response items."[54]

11

11 - What Common Core Means for Our Children

According to Dean Kalahar from the American Thinker, the foundational philosophy of Common Core is to create students ready for social action so they can force a social-justice agenda. He says Common Core is not about students who actually have a grasp of the intricate facts of a true set of what E.D. Hirsch would call "core knowledge."[55]

Common Core is about, as David Feith, assistant editor at The Wall Street Journal, would say, "an obsession with race, class, gender and sexuality as the forces of history and political identity."[56] He continues, "Nationalizing education via Common Core is about promoting an agenda of anti-capitalism, sustainability, white guilt, global citizenship, self-esteem, affective math, and culture sensitive spelling and language. This is done in the name of consciousness raising, moral relativity, fairness, diversity, and multiculturalism."

It all sounds very familiar and in line with a Progressive worldview. Some would say it is indoctrination through propaganda in our educational system. Education is used as the vehicle for social transformation.

According to Dave Hodges, award-winning psychologist, statistics and research professor who writes for The Daily Sheeple, the undeniable truth is that Common Core has the ulterior design on what should be taught to our children. He says that brainwashing our children is the ultimate goal of Common Core:

> Common Core is based upon social justice, arriving at knowledge and subsequent decision making through a spirit of collectivism and developing a communal agreement about the need to teach and to integrate into each classroom an underlying theme of sustainable development. These goals are not just going to be taught in specific Environmental Science courses, but these philosophies are to be implemented and taught in EACH and EVERY course that a child takes during their educational experiences

beginning with pre-K and stretching to post graduate secondary education.

Reform of the nation's standardized objectives is merely a smokescreen to the true intent of the program which is the acceptance for Agenda 21 policies. Subsequently, the Agenda 21/UNESCO documents clearly state their intention to turn each student into a globalist who will accept smaller living space, residing in the stack-and-pack cities of the future, acceptance of drastic energy reduction and the loss of Constitutional liberties.[57]

12

12 - Students Belong to the State/United Nations

Karen Schroeder, President of Advocates for Academic Freedom, warns us in her article "Common Core Standards Will Control You and Your Children":[58]

> The American educational system is being federalized through implementation of Race to the Top and Common Core Standards. Once Common Core Standards are completely implemented, the federal government will have total control of assessment tools and textbooks used in core subjects. Also, a national data collection system called State Longitudinal Data Systems (SLDS) will be used to determine a child's educational opportunities. The federalization of education will turn all school-choice programs into federally approved programs.
>
> The International Baccalaureate [IB] is a set of standards which are shaped by several United Nations treaties. International Baccalaureate Organization explains that IB and Common Core Standards share the values and beliefs of the UN's Universal Declaration of Human Rights with emphasis on Article 26.
>
> This means that Common Core Standards and IB programs are teaching beliefs and values contained in treaties that the United States does not support. Among these values are the surrender of the American Constitution, of national sovereignty, and of individual rights so students will accept becoming members of the "world community." The Common Core Standards focus on changing the social and political values of American children. Few goals address academics; math standards actually lower expectations. What had been required from a fourth grade student is now required from a fifth grader.
>
> The national data collection system (SLDS) will follow a child from Kindergarten to adulthood. A student's IQ scores, test scores, Social Security number, and medical records will become part of the collected data which will be used to help determine

> educational and job opportunities afforded each student.
>
> Once these systems are in place, all students in every educational setting will have to meet these state standards if they are going to pass the state-created assessment tools. Therefore, the education provided in every setting must include the curricula presented in state schools.
>
> To accomplish these goals, the federal government and the United Nations have cooperated to write textbooks that meet the goals of Common Core Standards and IB. The federal government is funding organizations that will create testing tools to assess the student's progress in accepting the social and political ideologies being taught in the classroom. Implementation of Common Core Standards is expected to be completed within the next two to three years.
>
> The only effective means of preventing international control of the American educational system is to eliminate the federal funding of education. An advocate for Academic Freedom is an educational consulting firm working with legislators across the United States to organize a conservative movement to eliminate federal control of education.
>
> Visit the Advocates for Academic Freedom home page, find the Petition for Progress button on the left side of the page, click on that button and sign the petition. To stop the federalization of education, we must have proof that there is sufficient support from the electorate. Please sign the petition and become a member of the grassroots movement to limit federal governmental control by removing federal funding of education and reallocating those funds to the states.

The idea that children belong to the state and not to their parents has been floating around in various circles for years. In a recent interview, Secretary of Education Arne Duncan advocated that schools should become "centers of community life" with longer days. The Obama administration has been promoting this with "cradle to career" initiatives.

Schools would be open 12 to 13 hours a day, 7 days a week; the schools would meet the social and emotional needs of students, and provide cultural and academic activities. To Duncan, such efforts are part of a "battle for social justice." If you are ready to relinquish all control of your children, this is the system for you. In a few years, the role of the family in the lives of your children would be greatly reduced.

13

13 - Legislative Action Dropping Common Core

Lindsey Burke from the Heritage Foundation recently reported that Indiana has given every state that adopted Common Core national standards and tests a lesson in prudent governance. Governor Mike Pence (R) signed the Common Core "Pause" bill into law, halting implementation of Common Core until state agencies, teachers and taxpayers fully study the implications of Common Core adoption.[59]

An article in Huff Post Politics entitled "Texas Ends CSCOPE Curriculum System after Concerns That It Had an Anti-American Agenda" was posted on May 21, 2013. Texas will discontinue the state-run curriculum system used by at least 875 of the state's school districts amid complaints that it contained lessons with an anti-American agenda.[60]

Conservative activists complained that its optional lessons promoted a "progressive pro-Islamic curriculum," according to the Texas Tribune. Activists took particular offense to one lesson that compared Boston Tea Party activists to terrorists and another that asked students to design a flag for a socialist country, reports the outlet.[61]

Furthermore, activists complained about the fact that many lesson plans were not available to the public. Without textbooks, lesson plans were online, and parents did not have access and therefore had no knowledge of what was being taught to their children. CSCOPE was in well over half of the schools in Texas and now it is being discontinued. This is a major victory for all of us fighting Common Core.

Twenty six of the states that have signed on to Common Core have segments of their population fighting Common Core. Some states have introduced legislation that has not passed and others have legislation in the wings.

People across America are just waking up to the Federal takeover of our education system. As parents become informed and legislators become educated, Common Core is being exposed for what it is and it is NOT American. We have no intention of letting the United Nations dictate to us what we should be teaching our children.

We say "United Nations" because this is not just a plan for the United States but for every country in the world. Common Core is just the beginning--involving control, uniform curriculum, data collection--of a bigger agenda to END freedom. Americans need to rise up and celebrate their heritage and pass our four sacred freedoms on to the next generation.

Senator Grassley sent a letter exhorting Congress to defund the federal government's role in the Common Core Standards and Curriculum. Eight senators joined Senator Grassley and signed onto the letter. They include Mike Lee (UT), Tom Coburn (OK), Jim Inhofe (OK), Deb Fischer (NE), Rand Paul (KY), Pat Roberts (KS), Jeff Sessions (AL), and Ted Cruz (TX).[62]

These senators understand that parents and teachers, not federal education bureaucrats, should decide how and what children learn. They understand that the Common Core has become a one-size-fits-all approach to education and that the federal government has no business using tax dollars to entice the states to adopt Common Core.

The Senate was not alone in opposing Common Core. Representative Blaine Luetkemeyer (MO) also circulated a letter to his colleagues in the House opposing Education Secretary Arne Duncan's support of Common Core, as well as the national databases which are threatening the privacy of children's data. Thirty-three other representatives also signed the letter.[63]

Hats off to Douglas County, Colorado where the school district and board of trustees get it! Brittany Corona in The Foundry reports that the school board rejected Common Core national standards due to the quality of the standards and on principle. They are not hood-winked into believing that these standards are home grown and want no part of distant national organizations or bureaucrats in Washington controlling what the students in Douglas County are taught.

> In the resolution, Douglas County school board members stated that it is their constitutional duty and discretion to set curriculum and standards for their students. They uphold that duty by using "broad local control to pursue world-class education innovations and the most rigorous academic standards anywhere—innovations and standards that will prepare our students for the demands of the 21st century workplace and global economy." They do not believe the Common Core standards allow them to uphold that duty or adequately prepare their students.
>
> In their list of grievances against the Common Core, the school board members stated that the Common Core is not appropriate for Douglas County because the district's current Guaranteed and Viable Curriculum (GVC) is "more rigorous, more thorough, and more directly tailored to the needs of Douglas County students" than the Common Core national standards.

> The members stated that "the District's leadership team has reviewed the Common Core Standards, and determined that they do not meet the expectations the District has for all of our students." The district leadership has been working alongside teachers for more than a year to create the GVC, and they believe that their locally grown curriculum will "best prepare our students for the college or career of their choice in the 21st century"—and that the Common Core will not.
>
> The members of the school board also voiced concern about the principle the national standards enforce: a top-down approach to education.
>
> The board officially resolved its "general opposition to a one-size-fits-all application of the Common Core Standards, because local school districts should retain broad latitude in establishing customized, rigorous and high standards and guidelines for the maximum educational attainment of all students in their specific communities."
>
> Douglas County is standing on the principle that local leaders, not Washington bureaucrats, ought to have control over what local students are being taught. They state, "Our taxpayers, parents, teachers and students expect the very highest and rigorous standards." The board plans to meet or exceed those expectations "at every turn, for every student, in every school." The best means to do that is to leave it in the hands of those who know their students best: parents and local leaders.[64]

In Michigan, Senator Tom McMillin, along with other colleagues, introduced HB 4276 which states, "The state board model core academic curriculum content standards shall not be based upon the Common Core Standards."[65] The bill is stalled in committee but that didn't stop McMillin. He and other House Republicans included a provision that prohibited Michigan Department of Education from funding Common Core implementation.

This is being touted as a playbook for defeating Common Core or at least holding it at bay until the public become educated as to what it is. Cutting the legs out from under it seems to be easier than amending state code.

This page left intentionally blank.

14 - Forces Converge to Defeat Common Core

Ben Velderman at EAGnews.org in Tallahassee tells us it is more than conservatives pushing back against Common Core. In his article, "Badass Teachers Association and other leftists join fight against Common Core" opponents are far from all being right-wing.

> BAT is a 25,000-member group of left-wing educators, union members and progressive activists who “are pushing back against the national (learning) standards with Twitter strikes, town hall meetings and snarky Internet memes,” reports Kathleen McGrory of the Miami Herald.
>
> Group members – known as BATs – share the concerns of conservatives and libertarians that Common Core will strip states and school districts of control over public education.
>
> BATs are also worried the one-size-fits-all learning standards for math and English place “too much emphasis on testing and will stifle creativity in the classroom,” McGrory reports.
>
> “The liberal critique of Common Core is that this is a huge profit-making enterprise that costs school districts a tremendous amount of money, and pushes out the things kids love about school, like art and music,” said Mark Nelson, a Fordham University professor and BAT co-founder.
>
> McGrory notes that the more traditional teachers union – the Florida Education Association – is also beginning to turn on Common Core.
>
> FEA President Andy Ford said some union members don’t like that their job reviews and (in some cases) wages will be determined by how well their students perform on assessments that are aligned with the new standards.

> They have a point. New York school districts switched to Common Core testing this spring and saw their students' test scores plummet.
>
> Education gadfly Diane Ravitch believes the Badass Teachers Association proves U.S. Education Secretary Arne Duncan is wrong when he "insists that the main criticism of Common Core comes from extremists and fringe groups like the Tea Party."
>
> McGrory notes "there are still plenty of Democrats who support the Common Core initiative, from the Obama administration down to teachers and parents on the local level. And in Florida, the movement still enjoys widespread support from the Republican-dominated legislature."
>
> "But the opposition is strong enough that state Sen. Dwight Bullard, D-Miami, is calling for a review before Florida moves further ahead with the standards and accompanying exams," McGrory writes.[66]

Senator Michael Watson in Mississippi is quoted as saying elected officials need to roll up their sleeves and get into the trenches on fighting Common Core before it is too late. In his own words:

> In a recent news report published in the Clarion Ledger on education, Lieutenant Governor Tate Reeves questions the timing of the inquiry into Common Core standards by myself and my colleagues in the Mississippi Senate Conservative Coalition. One might think based on his comments that bad policy has a statute of limitations by which it can no longer be challenged.
>
> I find that premise to be ludicrous. Mississippians don't want more political positioning, they want solutions, and as more information is made available we are finding that Common Core is not the solution for Mississippi. As is often the case, it is another example of government creating more complex problems.
>
> The Lt. Governor was quoted in the article as saying: "For those individuals who were in the Legislature four years ago, who didn't say anything but now decided they are going to complain — shame on them."
>
> Had the Lt. Governor asked someone who was in the legislature in 2010 before making such a reckless charge, he would have found that a vast majority of the legislature had never heard of Common Core.
>
> Not only was I in the Legislature four years ago, but I also sat on the Senate Education committee. I know we never discussed Common Core in the committee and I don't even remember the term "Common Core" being mentioned. So, let me make it clear that the Legislature never discussed Common Core, much less voted on it.

It sounds as if the Lieutenant Governor believes just because something is adopted by the Board of Education it becomes untouchable and beyond review. I certainly think not. My constituents elected me to represent them fully. I am not beholden to unelected bureaucrats' ideas of 'progress', and take seriously my responsibility of oversight.

We have a window of opportunity to talk candidly about real education solutions in Mississippi. The Mississippi Senate Conservative Coalition has decided to do so and has met with teachers, superintendents and parents from across the state to launch the conversation.

It's unfortunate that some in leadership refuse to protect the rights of Mississippi parents, and to protect the privacy of Mississippi children. It's also unfortunate that some in the Mississippi Legislature will stand idly by and allow the Department of Education to divest themselves of their mission, while having the temerity to demand more money to pay for administrative salaries that have no positive effect on the classroom.

Any legislator or legislative leader willing to sacrifice the duty of oversight and the education of our children out of personal political trepidation should allow someone else who is willing to do the hard work take their place.

I've spent six years debating the need for competition in education to pass public charter schools legislation. To watch the fruits of that labor negated by a one-size-fits-all national testing experiment is unthinkable and irresponsible.

Elected leaders who do not take this time to fully digest the reality of the situation and develop a plan that works to the benefit of Mississippi students will invite plenty of shame. I do not intend to be among that number.

There are many things we can do to develop the highest education standards right here in Mississippi without dependence on a consortium of bureaucrats with no responsibility towards or understanding of the unique needs of the people of our state. We have some of the best educators in the country here in Mississippi, and numerous examples of the highest standards in every discipline. I know this because I met with seven of our finest teachers, board members and administrators yesterday, and have talked to many more in the last two months.

The Mississippi Senate Conservative Coalition will look closely at solutions for Mississippi parents, students and teachers. Decades of allowing bureaucracy to reign unchecked and without serious questions have gotten us to this point. We must stop looking for a federal rescue, or the latest fad in policy or bureaucratic formulas to save us. We must begin taking seriously our responsibility to address these problems with courage, hard work and tenacity, and we can and should bring out the best Mississippi has to offer to do it.

> Some politicians need to roll up their sleeves and get in the trenches with us instead of sticking with the status quo and saying, "it's too late".
>
> If elected officials can't make that commitment–"shame on them".[67]

There are lots of reasons for hope. Common Core, along with many years of progressive indoctrination in our educational system, has to be turned around. Defeating Common Core is just part of our mission.

15 - CSCOPE vs. Common Core

On the website, The Right Planet, in her article "CSCOPE Is Common Core and It Isn't Good,"[68] Sara Noble tells us CSCOPE and Common Core are one and the same. Noble says they are both about micromanaging teachers and dumbing down students. Quoting from Ms. Noble:

> If you look at the curriculum, you will quickly see that the shift is from a nation founded on principles of liberty and justice to one founded on principles of pillage, bondage and imperialism. The only ones who stand up against the corrupt system are the Progressives aka Socialists and Communists.

The Daily Caller recently summarized ten of the shocking things in the Texas version of Common Core--namely, CSCOPE:[69]

- Islam and Mohammed are awesome. There are merits to the hijab. They present the hijab as “freeing” though its purpose is to hide women so they don’t tempt men. The curriculum is PC. They ignore the terrorism in Islam to promote the good.
- Christianity is a cult. They are guilty of grave atrocities
- Communism is awesome with all its big ideas
- Communism is awesome with all its big ideas.
- Making Communist flags is great.
- The Boston Tea Party was terrorism.
- Terrorism has goals and prisoners who have tried to kill Americans need more rights.

- Christopher Columbus warred against the land and ecology. He was an eco-terrorist.
- Paul Revere was evil and was suspected of drug involvement.
- Support for the Marxist U.N., and their global vision of population control is elevated.
- Murder and extortion were protest strategies of the Black Panthers.

16

16 - Is Common Core a Part of U.N. Agenda 21?

Rosa Koire says you won't see Common Core called Agenda 21: "It won't come with flashing lights announcing that it's part of a global standardization program to inventory, monitor, and control every aspect of your life." It is her belief that this system creates people who will go along to get along, who will be 'good obedient citizens'. Koire concludes, "This is a top down federal/global system for pseudo-education and is a tremendous threat to our independence as individuals and as a nation."

The following article, "Agenda 21: Common Core is Institutionalized Terrorism," is on Rosa Koire's website, Democrats Against U.N. Agenda 21:

> I guess I flatter myself that it takes a lot to shock me, but I am shocked. I've been researching Oklahoma and took a look at the universities to see how Agenda 21 is manifesting there. Well, I got a pretty good idea by looking at the University of Central Oklahoma's website.
>
> Under "Strategic Plan, I found Vision 2020. This plan (can't they come up with an original name anywhere in the entire United States?) is a raw and naked view of what schooling is supposed to be under U.N. Agenda 21 using Common Core Standards.
>
> After lots of Delphi sessions at the University, they determined in January 2013 that education should disconnect the students' minds and personalities from their beliefs and values. And remember, this is after students have endured 12 years of K-12 indoctrination. The Vision statement for the University is the generic chest-beating 'We will be a top national metropolitan university.' Ok, good luck. Then, this is followed by the real statement: “all student experiences will be rooted in Transformative Learning so our graduates are productive, creative, ethical and engaged citizens and leaders who contribute to the intellectual, cultural, economic and social enhancement of their

> communities.
>
> What, I asked myself, is Transformative Learning? I know that the word Transform is code for destroy. In order to transform it the existing system must be broken--demolished--and rebuilt.
>
> Because I wanted a quick answer, I used Wikipedia and got what I was looking for. Like a sort of electro-shock treatment, students' minds are wrenched out of their existing beliefs, the beliefs they developed over years of living and thinking and experiencing with family and friends. Transformative Learning requires the student--no, let me say it: THE PATIENT--to go through a disorienting dilemma that could be created by a teacher in order to 'undo racist, sexist, and other oppressive attitudes.' According to this, learning should be intuitive and emotional rather than fact-based. The student should examine his or her beliefs and TRANSFORM through the bonding with other students.
>
> This is a psychological technique NOT a teaching method. This is a way to break down the personality and replace it with a manageable new respondent to stimuli. In fact, this is social and behavioral demolition. Common Core is EMOTIONAL TERRORISM.[70]

A recent post of May 15, 2013, on the website Republic Magazine includes this commentary on Common Core:

> If Common Core Curriculum is allowed to be instituted throughout the American public education system, then it will signal the beginning of an inevitable end. Common Core Curriculum consists of material and content authorized by the federal government and United Nations. This type of education will twist and pervert the history of our country for future generations. The heroic stories you and I grew up with in our formative years will be put on display as atrocities carried out by early Americans. Common Core Curriculum will also entice future generations to accept what is being offered as factual. It will also embody further fear mongering tactics which will eventually lead to less liberty for the individual and more power for the elected elite.[71]

17 - Responses to Common Core

Common Core is a tragedy. Wake up, America. Listen to these teachers. Some teach now; some have retired over Common Core. Each has spoken out and each needs to be heard. A number of early childhood educators said they were shocked when they read the standards. They said it appeared that whoever wrote the standards had no knowledge of childhood development or early childhood education.

Parents are voicing their frustration as they see their children needlessly suffer through high stakes testing. Pastors are demanding to be heard. Below is a heartfelt letter from a wonderful teacher to her former students telling them why she cannot teach anymore. A PhD from Bulgaria weighs in on the road America is taking implementing Common Core. He says the end result of Common Core will be fully socialized communistic education, entirely controlled by the government.

Read these letters and weep. There are hundreds more letters on the web expressing similar sentiments about Common Core. They are heartbreaking.

My Profession No Longer Exists

Gerald Conti's resignation letter published in The Washington Post)[72]

Data driven education seeks only conformity, standardization, testing and a zombie-like adherence to the shallow and generic Common Core

Creativity, academic freedom, teacher autonomy, experimentation and innovation are being stifled in a misguided effort to fix what is not broken in our system of public education and particularly not at Westhill.

The New York State United Teachers union has let down its membership by failing to mount a much more effective and vigorous campaign against this same costly and dangerous debacle… our own administration has been both uncommunicative and unresponsive to the concerns and needs of our staff and students…

This situation has been exacerbated by other actions of the administration, in either refusing to call open forum meetings to discuss these pressing issues, or by so constraining the time limits of such meetings that little more than a conveying of information could take place. This lack of leadership at every level has only served to produce confusion, a loss of confidence and a dramatic and rapid decaying of morale.

The repercussions of these ill-conceived policies will be telling and shall resound to the detriment of education for years to come. The analogy that this process is like building the airplane while we are flying would strike terror in the heart of anyone should it be applied to an actual airplane flight, a medical procedure, or even a home repair. Why should it be acceptable in our careers and in the education of our children?

My profession is being demeaned by a pervasive atmosphere of distrust, dictating that teachers cannot be permitted to develop and administer their own quizzes and tests (now titled as generic "assessments") or grade their own students' examinations. The development of plans, choice of lessons and the materials to be employed are increasingly expected to be common to all teachers in a given subject. This approach not only strangles creativity, it smothers the development of critical thinking in our students and assumes a one-size-fits-all mentality more appropriate to the assembly line than to the classroom.

Teacher planning time has also now been so greatly eroded by a constant need to "prove up" our worth to the tyranny of APPR (through the submission of plans, materials and "artifacts" from our teaching) that there is little time for us to carefully critique student work, engage in informal intellectual discussions with our students and colleagues, or conduct research and seek personal improvement through independent study. We have become increasingly evaluation and not knowledge driven.

I am not leaving my profession, in truth, it has left me. It no longer exists. I feel as though I have played some game halfway through its fourth quarter, a timeout has been called, my teammates' hands have all been tied, the goal posts moved, all previously scored points and honors expunged and all of the rules altered.

The president of the College Board's recent announcement that a new SAT will be created to measure Common Core Standards skills proficiency also alarms us. In addition, the Secretary of Education's former press secretary has recently used the "revolving door" of public office to acquire a job with a company that is related to Pearson LLC.

Fear and Loathing and the Common Core

Posted on his Raginghoresblog on April 18, 2013[73]

This morning, like yesterday morning and the morning before that, I was complicit in the wholesale corporatization of American public school education, playing my small but essential role in a corporate experiment of unprecedented proportions and titanic intent. This morning and yesterday morning and the morning before that, I, like thousands of my fellow teachers, administered to my students the first of a promised endless battery of New York State standardized tests.

It is hard not to feel demoralized if not utterly invisible administering such things, that much the more when you know that few in your profession had any say at all in the production of such things, that such tests are incapable of measuring and therefore subtly dismiss the most sublime human gifts such as creativity, and that they are designed, in large part, to strip teachers of our autonomy.

And more than that: you know that under the current data crazed evaluation systems, the outcomes of such these tests threaten your very livelihood.

It is harder still to believe that such emotions are not part of the design of the entire project. After all, a cowed, terrified workforce is a compliant workforce and no word is more operative in today's "new normal" school system than "compliance."

The Pearson produced tests are all aligned to what are deceitfully called the Common Core State Standards, the first of countless tests to be so, and as such are designed to insure the ten year olds in my charge were on track to be "college and career ready", the better to help them succeed in the global economy and "win the future."

And who can argue with that?

I can.

I can because not only is such a notion of education limited and limiting to the point of vulgarity, but because everything about the Common Core State Standards Initiative, beginning with its name, stinks to high heaven. Everything about this privately funded, privately owned, secretly created scheme, sponsored by the un-elected National Governors Association and given pseudo academic legitimacy by the equally unelected but lofty sounding Council Of Chief State School Officers, is meant to obscure or hide altogether what the Common Core is, why it exists and how it came, ready or not, to be rammed down the throat of almost every school kid in America including the ten year olds I saw pointlessly suffer through it the past three days.

Search the New York State Education website and you will find nothing about the Core's (as it is now called) main funders, Bill and Melinda Gates, nothing about its fantastically lucrative connection to Pearson Publishing, who have already made millions and stand to reap billions of tax payer bucks creating more tests for our kids, beginning in kindergarten, than have ever been seen before in human history, nothing about the multimillion dollar Common Core paraphernalia industry.

Lord of American Education

Seek and you will find nothing to indicate the “Core”, in Common Core is, in fact, nothing less than the arbitrary selections of educational entrepreneur and non-teacher, David Coleman, pal of Michelle Rhee; he , who gets to pretty much single handedly decide what is and what is not important in our children’s education.

The Divine Decider

And this does he, from sea to shining sea.

Seek and you will find nothing about the grossly coercive manner in which the Obama administration forced the Common Core upon cash starved states in exchange for their autonomy and enough strings attached to slowly strangle their teacher unions who insanely went along with it; nothing about the totalitarian ethic inherent in the Core that mandates that once “adopted (what a disgracefully manipulative use of our language!) by a state not a single comma of the holy document could be altered.

Seek and you will find nothing to indicate the fact the “initiative” in the Common Core State Standard Initiative is the initiative not of states, teachers or parents, but only that of its super rich sponsors and corporations. Seek and you will find nothing about the incredible fact that the vast experiment called the Common Core has never even been field-tested even as it is utterly remaking the American public school system as we breathe.

What kind of people would do this?

Nothing I can think of in the current political landscape more clearly illuminates the insidious transformation of the United States from a problematic democracy into an outright oligarchy and corporate fiefdom than the remarkable series of outrageous experiments currently being performed on American public school children at the behest of a handful of unelected, wholly unaccountable, madly narcissistic billionaires and their corporate allies via the machinations of their hirelings in elected office. As yet, the most outrageous of these experiments is the Common Core and its concomitant testing frenzy than comes with it. As many have pointed out, the children of the proponents of the Common Core go to schools that hold such stuff in outright disdain.

We should do as well. Those intrepid parents in the Opt Out movement are showing the way. The testing industry is the central nervous system of the entire corporate education reform campaign. If enough refuse to feed it, it will die. If we continue to accept it, our already deeply enfeebled democracy will.

Next year my child will enter "a testing grade" and is therefore meant to share in the glories of the Common Core Initiative. Let me rephrase that: She will be forced to share in the glories of the Common Core Initiative.

Note: as they are expanding their empire to kindergarten, next year just about everyone's child is meant to share in the glories of the Common Core State Standard Initiative.

I do not know what will happen from now till then but I know this: My child will partake in this ruthless, rapacious corporate hustle over my dead body.

A Wyoming School's Common Core Gag Order

Filed in Common Core State Standards by Shane Vander Hart on April 24, 2013. This email was received from a 6th grade teacher in Wyoming. Her name is withheld to protect her privacy.[74]

I am currently a teacher in a smaller district in Wyoming. I attended a Wyoming Department of Education training for the ELA Common Core Standards in July, prior to starting the 2012/2013 school year. I came to this training knowing only that Wyoming, along with 45 others states were choosing to adopt the standards fully by 2015. The WDE presenters were suggesting we use some of the methods I had been trained to use in Utah, and had previously used when I taught there. Since our state and district benchmarks would not be fully aligned with textbooks, curriculum, and testing until 2015, I wanted to get a head start.

I looked into what my former colleagues were doing in Utah. This is when I discovered the movement that 2 Moms from Utah and Christel Swasey have been a HUGE part of. I was FLOORED! I had no idea that there was a different train of thought, let alone a movement against the implementation of Common Core.

This peaked my curiosity and caused me to do some researching. I quickly realized how ignorant I really was about our country's education system and how the Department of Education affects what happens in our schools. It was truly ignorance on my part, as I only saw how things happened on a local level and never really thought about the effects of national legislation affecting a small town in Wyoming.

The more I researched the more I become aware of how much I didn't know! I also began forming my own opinions about how this could potentially limit local voices from parents, teachers, and administrators. I chose to share my research and opinions with my administrator and a few close colleagues privately. I emailed links to the research I'd done, along with my views on what is happening and how it could potentially affect us as parents, and teachers. After the email was sent I met one-on-one with my administrator, where we discussed Common Core and the research I had done and continue to do. Basically, I left that meeting knowing that he disagreed with what my opinion is. However, I left with the feeling that we would agree to disagree. He also pointed out the fact that our state and district would be moving forward with Common Core and I would need to be on board with it.

The next day I was approached by a fellow teacher whom I'd shared my concerns with. They asked if I would be comfortable sharing those same concerns during a grade level meeting, as others were curious. I agreed to do so. During the meeting I spoke of several movements in various states that are pushing to repeal the adoption of Common Core, or at least give more time to consider it. I spoke of being shocked that I was ignorant of any controversy surrounding the Common Core. I shared my feelings, concerns and opinions. I suggested they become aware that there are two sides to this and to be prepared to have an opinion. I pointed out that questions could come from concerned parents or others in the community. I also shared that my main concern was with the changes to data privacy and losing local control. When I was finishing my administrator said that there would be no more emailing, or talking about the Common Core amongst the staff. There was finality to his tone and the meeting was quickly over at that point. I then received an email from my administrator reminding me of our district policy of not using school resources to push political concerns or agendas. He also stated that there was to be no more discussion about Common Core unless it was on an "educational" basis between staff members.

Ironically, I had several teachers contact me outside of school that same day, to say they were shocked at my administrators tone. They felt I was being genuine in sharing information that was previously unknown and could potentially affect educators. Several staff member have also approached me saying that they are grateful for this information and are now researching it on their own.

The question being asked in my school now is…Why can't educators do what they do best? Research, question, inform?? Isn't it better to question and discuss things, even if we don't agree on them as to find what is best for the children we have been entrusted with? Should we turn a blind eye, and be lead like sheep off the cliff?

What is wrong with forming an opinion, discussing it, whether we agree with each other or not? Why stifle this? I don't think he realized that he just gave fuel to what was once a single voice!

At this point my union representatives are looking into this as a form of suppressing free speech. I also have an appointment set up to meet with our district's superintendent so that I may better understand the position our district is going to take on this. At this point the staff at my school believes they will be reprimanded if they speak with parents concerning Common Core for something other than its educational use.

(You might want to Google this article. The 16 comments following the article are revealing as to what is going on with teachers.)

A tough critique of Common Core on early childhood education

By Valerie Strauss, Published: January 29, 2013 on The Answer Sheet.[75]

The debate on the Common Core State Standards has in recent months centered on the issue of how much fiction high school students should read. Here's a tough critique on the standards and how they relate to early childhood education. It was written by Edward Miller, a writer and teacher who lives in Wellfleet, Massachusetts. He is the co-author of "Crisis in the Kindergarten: Why Children Need to Play in School." By Edward Miller and Nancy Carlsson-Paige

Recent critiques of the Common Core Standards by Marian Brady and John T. Spencer have noted that the process for creating the new K-12 standards involved too little research, public dialogue, or input from educators.

Nowhere was this more startlingly true than in the case of the early childhood standards—those imposed on kindergarten through grade 3. We reviewed the makeup of the committees that wrote and reviewed the Common Core Standards. In all, there were 135 people on those panels. Not a single one of them was a K-3 classroom teacher or early childhood professional.

It appears that early childhood teachers and child development experts were excluded from the K-3 standards-writing process.

When the standards were first revealed in March 2010, many early childhood educators and researchers were shocked. "The people who wrote these standards do not appear to have any background in child development or early childhood education," wrote Stephanie Feeney of the University of Hawaii, chair of the Advocacy Committee of the National Association of Early Childhood Teacher Educators.

The promoters of the standards claim they are based in research. They are not. There is no convincing research, for example, showing that certain skills or bits of knowledge (such as counting to 100 or being able to read a certain number of words) if mastered in kindergarten will lead to later success in school. Two recent studies show that direct instruction can actually limit young children's learning. At best, the standards reflect guesswork, not cognitive or developmental science.

Moreover, the Common Core Standards do not provide for ongoing research or review of the outcomes of their adoption—a bedrock principle of any truly research-based endeavor.

It's bad enough to set up committees to make policy on matters they know little or nothing about. But it's worse to conceal and distort the public reaction to those policies. And that's exactly what happened.

Take a look at the summary of "public feedback" posted on the Core Standards website. It is grossly misleading. First of all, calling the feedback "public" is wrong: the organizers of the standards would not make public the nearly 10,000 comments they say they received from citizens. The summary quotes 24 respondents–less than 1/4 of 1 percent of the total–selectively chosen to back up their interpretation of the results.

Reading this summary, one gets the clear impression that the reactions to the standards were overwhelmingly positive. "At least three-fourths of educators, from pre-kindergarten through higher education, reacted positively or very positively to each of the general topics," reports the section on the math standards. The summary concludes: "The feedback is, overall, very good news for the standards developers."

Early childhood gets few mentions in this summary. The first one, on page 3, quotes an anonymous respondent: "Add pre-k standards." In other words, not only do educators supposedly like the K-3 standards, they want them pushed down to even younger children. (In fact, that's what's happening now in many states.)

The authors of the summary do say that a "group of respondents believe the [K-3] standards are developmentally inappropriate." They characterize that group as being mainly parents who are concerned that "children are being pushed too hard."

But they don't even mention a critically important statement opposing the K-3 standards, signed by more than 500 early childhood professionals. The Joint Statement of Early Childhood Health and Education Professionals on the Common Core Standards Initiative were signed by educators, pediatricians, developmental psychologists, and researchers, including many of the most prominent members of those fields.

Their statement reads in part:

We have grave concerns about the core standards for young children.... The proposed standards conflict with compelling new research in cognitive science, neuroscience, child development, and early childhood education about how young children learn, what they need to learn, and how best to teach them in kindergarten and the early grades.

The statement's four main arguments, below, are grounded in what we know about child development; facts that all education policymakers need to be aware of:

1. The K-3 standards will lead to long hours of direct instruction in literacy and math. This kind of "drill and grill" teaching has already pushed active, play-based learning out of many kindergartens.

2. The standards will intensify the push for more standardized testing, which is highly unreliable for children under age eight.

3. Didactic instruction and testing will crowd out other crucial areas of young children's

learning: active, hands-on exploration, and developing social, emotional, problem-solving, and self-regulation skills—all of which are difficult to standardize or measure but are the essential building blocks for academic and social accomplishment and responsible citizenship.

4. There is little evidence that standards for young children lead to later success. The research is inconclusive; many countries with top-performing high-school students provide rich play-based, nonacademic experiences—not standardized instruction—until age six or seven.

The National Association for the Education of Young Children is the foremost professional organization for early education in the U.S. Yet it had no role in the creation of the K-3 Core Standards. The Joint Statement opposing the standards was signed by three past presidents of the NAEYC—David Elkind, Ellen Galinsky, and Lilian Katz—and by Marcy Guddemi, the executive director of the Gesell Institute of Human Development; Dr. Alvin Rosenfeld of Harvard Medical School; Dorothy and Jerome Singer of the Yale University Child Study Center; Dr. Marilyn Benoit, past president of the American Academy of Child and Adolescent Psychiatry; Professor Howard Gardner of the Harvard Graduate School of Education; and many others.

We know that the instigators of the standards at the National Governors Association and the Council of Chief State School Officers were aware of the Joint Statement well before their summary of public feedback was written. Copies of it were hand-delivered to eleven officials at those two organizations, including Gene Wilhoit, executive director of the CCSSO, and Dane Linn, director of the Education Division of the NGA, who were primarily responsible for the creation of the standards.

We called Mr. Wilhoit and Mr. Linn (who is now vice president of the Business Roundtable), along with several other people involved in the process, to ask them to comment for this article on the way the public feedback summary and the K-3 standards themselves were written. None of them returned our calls.

Why were early childhood professionals excluded from the Common Core Standards project? Why were the grave doubts of our most knowledgeable education and health experts missing from the official record of this undertaking? Would including them have forced the people driving this juggernaut to face serious criticism and questions about the legitimacy of the entire project?

The Common Core Standards are now the law in 46 states. But it's not too late to unearth the facts about how and why they were created, and to raise an alarm about the threat they represent.

The stakes are enormous. Dr. Carla Horwitz of the Yale Child Study Center notes that many of our most experienced and gifted teachers of young children are giving up in despair. "They are leaving the profession," says Horwitz, "because they can no longer do what they know will ensure learning and growth in the broadest, deepest way. The Core Standards will cause suffering, not learning, for many, many young children."

Our first task as a society is to protect our children. The imposition of these standards endangers them. To learn more about how early childhood educators are working to defend young children, see Defending the Early Years.

Principal: 'I was naïve about Common Core'

Posted by Valerie Strauss on March 4, 2013 on The Answer Sheet.[76]

It's a powerful piece about how an award-winning principal went from being a Common Core supporter to an opponent. Carol Burris was named the 2010 New York State Outstanding Educator by the School Administrators Association in New York State. She is one of the co-authors of the principals' letter against evaluating teachers by student test scores, which was signed by 1,535 New York principals.)

When I first read about the Common Core State Standards, I cheered. I believe that our schools should teach all students (except for those who have severe learning disabilities), the skills, habits and knowledge that they need to be successful in post-secondary education. That doesn't mean that every teenager must be prepared to enter Harvard, but it does mean that every young adult, with few exceptions, should at least be prepared to enter their local community college. That is how we give students a real choice.

I even co-authored a book, "Opening the Common Core," on how to help schools meet that goal. It is a book about rich curriculum and equitable teaching practices, not about testing and sanctions. We wrote it because we thought that the Common Core would be a student-centered reform based on principles of equity.

I confess that I was naïve. I should have known in an age in which standardized tests direct teaching and learning, that the standards themselves would quickly become operationalized by tests. Testing, coupled with the evaluation of teachers by scores, is driving its implementation. The promise of the Common Core is dying and teaching and learning are being distorted. The well that should sustain the Core has been poisoned.

I hear about those distortions every day. Many of the teachers in my high school are also the parents of young children. They come into my office with horror stories regarding the incessant pre-testing, testing and test prep that are taking place in their own children's classrooms. Last month, a colleague gave me a multiple-choice quiz taken by his seven-year old son during music. Here is a question:

Kings and queens COMMISSIONED Mozart to write symphonies for celebrations and ceremonies. What does COMMISSION mean?

1. to force someone to do work against his or her will

2. to divide a piece of music into different movements

3. to perform a long song accompanied by an orchestra

4. to pay someone to create artwork or a piece of music

Whether or not learning the word ‘commission’ is appropriate for second graders could be debated. I personally think it is a bit over the top. What is of deeper concern, however, is that during a time when 7 year olds should be listening to and making music, they are instead taking a vocabulary quiz.

I think that the reason for the quiz is evident to anyone who has been following the reform debate. The Common Core places an extraordinary emphasis on vocabulary development. Probably, the music teacher believes she must do her part in test prep. More than likely she is being evaluated in part by the English Language Arts test scores of the building. Teachers are engaged in practices like these because they are pressured and afraid, not because they think the assessments are educationally sound. Their principals are pressured and nervous about their own scores and the school’s scores. Guaranteed, every child in the class feels that pressure and trepidation as well.

An English teacher in my building came to me with a ‘reading test’ that her third grader took. Her daughter did poorly on the test. As both a mother and an English teacher she knew that the difficulty of the passage and the questions were way over grade level. Her daughter, who is an excellent reader, was crushed. She and I looked on the side of the copy of the quiz and found the word “Pearson.” The school, responding to pressure from New York State, had purchased test prep materials from the company that makes the exam for the state.

I am troubled that a company that has a multi-million dollar contract to create tests for the state should also be able to profit from producing test prep materials. I am even more deeply troubled that this wonderful little girl, whom I have known since she was born, is being subject to this distortion of what her primary education should be.

There are so many stories that I could tell–the story of my guidance counselor’s sixth-grade, learning disabled child who feels like a failure due to constant testing, a principal of an elementary school who is furious with having to use to use a book he deems inappropriate for third graders because his district bought the State Education Department approved common core curriculum, and the frustration of math teachers due to the ever-changing rules regarding the use of calculators on the tests. And all of this is mixed with the toxic fear that comes from knowing you will be evaluated by test results and that “your score” will be known to any of your parents who ask.

When state education officials chide, “Don’t drill for the test, it does not work”, teachers laugh. Of course test prep works. Every parent who has ever paid hundreds of dollars for SAT prep knows it works, but no parent is foolish enough to think that the average 56 point ‘coaching’ jump in an SAT score means that their child is more “college ready.”

Test scores are a rough proxy for learning. Tests imperfectly examine selected domains of skills, so that we can infer what students know. Real learning occurs in the mind of the learner when she makes connections with prior learning, makes meaning, and retains that knowledge in order to create additional meaning from new information. In short, with tests we see traces of learning, not learning itself.

What occurs in a “data driven”, high-stakes learning environment is that the full domain of what should be learned narrows to those items tested. The Common Core, for example, wants students to grow in five skill areas in English Language Arts — reading, writing, speaking, listening and collaboration. But the Common Core tests will only measure reading and writing. Parents can expect that the other three will be neglected as teachers frantically try to prepare students for the difficult and high-stakes tests. What gets measured gets done, and make no mistake: “reformers” understand that full well. In fact, they count on it. They see data, not children. For the corporate reformers, test data constitute the bottom-line profits that they watch.

There is no one more knowledgeable about school change and systemic reforms than Michael Fullan. He is a renowned international authority on school reform, having been actively engaged in both its implementation as well in the analysis of reform results. I had the pleasure of listening to him this week at the Long Island ASCD spring conference.

Fullan told us that the present reforms are led by the wrong drivers of change, individual accountability of teachers, linked to test scores and punishment, cannot be successful in transforming schools. He told us that the Common Core standards will fall of their own weight because standards and assessments, rather than curriculum and instruction are driving the Common Core. He explained that the right driver of school change is capacity building. Data should be used as a strategy for improvement, not for accountability purposes. The Common Core is a powerful tool, but it is being implemented using the wrong drivers.

Fullan helped to successfully lead the transformation of schools in Ontario, Canada, and he has tried to influence our national conversation, but his advice has been shunned. I will close with a final quote from Fullan and let readers draw their own conclusions:

A fool with a tool is still a fool. A fool with a powerful tool is a dangerous fool.

by Carol Burris

Missouri Mom Shares Common Core Horror Story

Letter sent from parent to Karen Bracken at Tennessee Against Common Core.[77]

I first started my crusade against the sick practices in education about four years ago in our community when my son would bring home math with every single correct answer on his math work sheet counted wrong...even though every answer was right. I learned then, that it was about the process, not about the answer. I was perplexed. I had a million questions, but no one would answer my questions. Therefore, I was labeled as one of "those" moms. My son's principal told me that he would not be memorizing any math facts because (and I quote): "To memorize math facts is a waste of brain power. We are a generation of cell phones and calculators, those skills are not needed and it is a waste." I was stunned. I walked away telling my friends that this fight had nothing to do with math. I did not know what it was about then, but I KNEW that it was much bigger than math.

My daughter was punished as a 5th grader for just answering questions like "5x8=40" She was told that she HAD to draw the 40 stick people in order to "SHOW" that she knew what she was doing. She was asked by her teacher, "do you want to do it the old fashioned way, or the RIGHT way?" She was not allowed to be the fastest and most efficient problem solver. She was forced to insult her intelligence and draw silly pictures and "arrays" in order to show she understood the process. Quickly I learned that math was not about numbers any more. It was not about right answers any more. It was about teaching in a way that no parent understood, but many were convinced to "trust" that this new way was so much better. Many (and I will apologize in advance, but it is an accurate depiction of what I believe I see in Missouri and an actual term that is applicable to all that we see right now in our nation) "useful idiots" would parrot the ridiculousness that would just leave me wanting to kick box my way out of those ridiculous "math nights" my school district hosted in an effort to convince parents they knew what they were doing. I was never convinced. In fact I was insulted.

As I started to make more and more noise, the grading system was quickly changed. Every child was all of a sudden getting an "A". People would apologize that my kids did not "get it" but, would tell me that their children were doing better than they had ever done before; they were all of a sudden getting an "A". Heck, everyone was. The honor roll was littering the pages of our newspaper every quarter, yet no one thought that to be odd. Parents were told not to try to help their children because they would only confuse them. The hair on the back on my neck would stand up when school officials would say that to me. My children were in elementary school and I was not an idiot. I COULD help my child, but I quickly learned that was not allowed. I realized at that point that it was more about keeping our children thinking that their parents were not smart enough to help them...they were being taught that we were too old fashioned. They were being taught to value the school and what their teachers were teaching them more than anything they could get at home. It was creepy. Again, it was more than math. I just could not see the whole picture yet.

I pulled my sons out of school when I was told that during my son's free time, which he had for an hour a day, he could not practice the standard algorithm in a workbook that was aligned to the Missouri "Grade Level Expectations" (GLEs). He would come home and tell me that kids were reading Stephen King novels, reading Popular Mechanic, playing on the computer, drawing pictures, doing whatever they wanted if they did not need interventions (which he never did), but they would not allow for him to work in a work book that we practiced in every evening with him to hone his math skills. His teacher was so nervous when she had to tell us not to send the workbook back because it was not allowed. When I would ask her, why she would just very nervously plead with me not to be mad with her, she did not know, nor did she find any harm in it. My husband and I went to the principal and asked why. No answer. We went to the superintendent and asked why. No answer. We wrote letters to the school board and asked why. Never any answers.

Today, the dots have been connected. I see the picture clearly. My school has been piloting the Common Core material for the past three years. The data collection and the shutting out of parents make total sense now. I am not a mom who ever believed that I would be home schooling my children. However, what I see happening in our schools is educational malpractice, and I could not live with myself if I did not find a way to make sure that my children got the educational foundation that they deserve. I am certainly not a teacher. I would have never believed that I was equipped to do be their teacher. However, I am convinced that I cannot do them more damage than is being done to millions of children on a daily basis in this country. I am convinced that this mom with the ability to read, and a little common sense is far more equipped to reach my kids than any current day teacher is allowed to with what is being forced upon the teachers in public schools today.

I am sick of the "big business" of education. I am sick of my children being viewed as data. I am sick of their hopes and dreams ignored while they are the guinea pigs in the perpetual experiments in education being conducted every single day at their expense and ours. They have hopes and dreams. They have little beating hearts and souls. They are so much more than the data they are viewed as. They have bright futures if we do not allow for the government and the chosen few to strip those dreams from them. I am honored to stand with you in this fight. I say that we swing for the fences. I won't go down without a valiant fight for my children and yours. Happy to feel like we can make a difference. Happy to stand with you all united for this great cause.

Oklahoma Pastors' Letter Against Common Core

[78]February 19, 2013

To the Honorable:

Governor Mary Fallin
Lieutenant Governor Todd Lamb
State School Superintendent Janet Barresi
Members of the Oklahoma Legislature

The most concerning thing about last November's Presidential election was not the outcome, but that almost 60 million people thought reelecting Barak Obama was a good idea. How did a man who openly supports unfettered abortion, homosexual marriage, record setting deficit spending and the redistribution of wealth garner the support of nearly 60 million voters? The reason: That is what the voters have been taught in an educational system that is controlled by the Federal Government.

Beginning with LBJ's Elementary and Secondary Education Act, the Federal Government began an unconstitutional power grab over public education. Then in 1991, President George H. W. Bush tied American education into the standards set by the United Nations Education Scientific and Cultural Organization. Since then, every few years the Federal government rolls out the latest version of the same old UN standards. Whether you call it Goals 2000, No Child Left Behind, Race to the Top, or Core Curriculum it's the same old junk and we keep buying it.

The Founder's design was for local control of education. Unfortunately, the school busses in my town still say "Edmond Public Schools", but they really aren't. They are the Edmond branch of an educational system controlled by Washington D.C. We voluntarily have sold our freedom for the sake of funds that come from a bankrupt government, that forces conservative, God fearing Oklahoma children to abide by the government mandated curriculum which is birthed by UNESCO with the intent on creating a sustainable earth without borders.

We have kicked God out of school and replaced Him with Darwin and Marx. If there is no God, then government is the grantor of all rights including my Obamaphone and Obamacare. That is why American Exceptionalism is no longer taught, but evil American Imperialism is.

Rather than teaching our kids to be thrifty, hardworking and self-reliant, we are taught government dependency. Since God doesn't exist, there is no absolute truth and consequently right and wrong has been replaced with tolerance and intolerance. We are taught that Islam is good and Christianity is bad. We are not taught to be good citizens (as our founders demanded) we are taught to be global citizens. We are taught about "rights", but we aren't taught responsibility. We aren't taught that no one has a right to do wrong.

Core Curriculum may be the most dangerous Trojan horse that has yet been brought to our gates for the following reason. With the new push toward the [Common] Core Curriculum Standards, the ACT and SAT tests are adjusting to reflect those same standards. All text books will then conform to these new standards as even "homeschool" and "private school" will be forced to be taught to the test. If we do not stop this program now, it will become America's next Medicare or Social Security and millions of children will be lost inside a one size fits all system to create equal mediocrity among the new "global citizens."

Let's restore American exceptionalism and reject the [Common] Core Curriculum. We're smart enough to make decisions about our own children and our own schools. Let's return Oklahoma Schools to Oklahoma control.

Sincerely,(Fifty some pastors in Oklahoma signed this letter.)

To My Students: 'I Love You and Believe in You'

By Kris Nielsen, a 7th grade teacher in Georgia[79]

This is why we are going to defeat Common Core in our schools. There are enough wonderful teachers working with our children who will take a stand and say we will not be a part of doing this to our children. - Marian Armstrong

To My Students,

I did not return to the classroom this year and I want to apologize. I am truly sorry for having left you. It was the hardest decision I have ever made. I want you to understand why I left. It had nothing to do with you. I still love you and believe in you. You are still amazing and you can do anything you want to do. I did not give up on you. I left to fight for you.

I saw you struggling with Common Core skills. Even with the new curriculum from the district, no matter how I broke it down for you I could see you didn't understand. I saw the frustration on your faces. And when time ran out and we had to take the county's test (on the county's schedule), I saw the tears roll from your eyes. You failed. I saw you missing school more days than normal. I saw you with long sleeves covering up the cutting scars on your arms. I saw how the sparkle in your eyes dimmed. I saw the small bald spot on your head where you had pulled out your hair. And it wasn't just in my class. You hated going to math. You came early every day for homework help, but it didn't make any difference. You still could not understand.

I want you to know none of this is your fault. It is not you. I know the school, the county and the state call it "rigor." That is a horrible word. Look it up in the dictionary for me. Rigor is for dead people. You are not failing because it is too hard. You are not failing because you are not working hard enough. You are not failing because of your teachers. You are failing because Common Core was not written by teachers. Common Core was not written to help you. Let me explain why this hurts you so much.

Your brain, as it develops, can only learn certain things at certain times. Common Core is trying to force you to learn things your brain is not ready to learn. Researchers for decades have found that the things Common Core requires you to do are impossible until you reach high school, at the earliest. No matter what your teachers do to get you to learn it, you aren't going to be able to. There is nothing wrong with you. Your brain was designed perfectly. Common Core standards were not.

Common Core was written by businessmen trying to make money off of you. You and your learning are a grand experiment in corporate profits. If you fail at school, if your teachers fail to teach you, these corporations can sell more books, workbooks, tests, software and technology to schools and even to your parents to try at home. None of it will work. These same businessmen want to convince states to let them and their companies take over your schools. Your parent's tax dollars would then go to these companies. Over $600 billion is spent on education every year in this country. This money should go to your education, not to private companies. It is very similar to what was done to prisons several years ago.

Common Core is the first time in the history of this country that a privately written and copyrighted plan has become public policy. There is no research to back it and it has never been tested. Politicians are pushing it because these corporations are giving them money to push it.

When I left, I met with members of your Board of Education and told them what was happening. They ignored me. I went to the local newspaper and they ignored me too. When I spoke to the state Senate education committee they dismissed me as a political nut job. When I came back to chaperone your fall dance I was told I was "no longer one of you" and I could not come in because of my position on Common Core. Ghandi once said, "First they ignore you, then they ridicule you, then they fight you, and then you win." We will win. We will win for you and every student after you. This is not political. This is for the future leaders of our country. These corporations don't want to teach you how to think.

It is time for you to talk to your parents. Help them understand that opting you out of state testing will protect your personal information as well as stop the data that is being used to unfairly judge you and your teachers. Schools where more than 80% of kids have been opted out are cancelling these stressful tests that measure nothing. There is a new test coming to replace the CRCT, which is why politicians like Governor Deal and Superintendent Barge want to keep Common Core. Have your parents demand a portfolio of your work be kept and that your hard work be used to decide if you should go on to the next grade, not a random test. Any test not written by and graded by your teachers should never be allowed in the classroom.

Please do not worry about me. I am strong and people have called me worse names and banned me from much better places. Standing up for what is right is not always the easy thing. I knew that when I left my classroom. I have 32,000 other teachers from all over the country who are standing with me. I have education experts and child psychologists standing with me. I have politicians standing with me. I have famous authors standing with me. And the group is growing.

Just this week I got an email from Judy Blume, author of famous children's classics like Tales of a Fourth Grade Nothing, Blubber, Are You There God, It's Me Margaret, Forever, and Tiger Eyes. She shared with me that she was a horrible test-taker. She is very grateful that she is not in school taking the kinds of tests you are taking. Can you imagine how horrible it would be if our favorite authors gave up because they could not do well on standardized tests that meant nothing? I don't want to find out.

Talk to your parents and let them know what is happening in your classrooms. Every time you take a test or a survey, tell your parents. Be brave and keep making me proud. You can be anything you want to be. I am always here for you.

Mrs. Meg Norris, Ed.S.
7th Grade (former) teacher
Georgia

PhD from Bulgaria warns us of things to come if we don't wake up.

By Viktor Kostov[80]

The end result of the full application of the Common Core will be fully socialized communistic education, entirely controlled by the government.

This is not my partiality for "conservative values." I am speaking from the reality of post-communist Bulgaria (Eastern Europe). The state (government) Ministry of Education is the sole standard and source of ANY thought on the philosophy of education (or lack thereof). Private education is subject to the government's a) permission and b) curriculum. Homeschooling was unheard of until recently.

At a conversation with the chair of the parliamentarian commission on education last year I brought up the idea that the government-issued diploma should not be the sole verification of one's academic achievement. This was a novel idea to the gentleman -- he was sincerely amazed at the notion of a standardized test made up by educators unrelated to the state; and that the purpose of government education should be to provide an alternative for those who choose to, or cannot school their children privately or at home. He and even a "right wing" Bulgarian politician were stunned at the idea that a government school should not be a factory for citizens (as many European states see education).

Homeschooling here (Bulgaria), although now widely debated due to the latest events and our efforts, is still a largely non-existent category in the minds of the general public. The reason for this absence is in the worldview and the perception -- the god of the state provides knowledge for our children. For free. This thinking is a remainder from totalitarianism but is so deeply imbedded in the culture that any thought of education free from government control and intrusion is political and social heresy. And biblical heresy for most Christians here (until the debate started about a year ago with the Child Law).

While America is still relatively far off from fully aligning all education to a centralized government, which is the direction of the Common Core. However, the introduction of a globalist agenda and the push to socialism, so visible under the current federal government, will not let up any time soon in the U.S.

The issue of who controls education is deeply ideological, political, theological, value-based and worldview-based. It is a faith-issue and religious freedom issue. It is even a matter of who do we worship -- God or Caesar. Viktor Kostov, PhD

18

18 - Actions to Remove Common Core

Educate Parents

If after reading this book you are convinced of the dangers of Common Core, do not give up. Become educated. Join with other parents. Talk to your children's teachers and principal. Know your rights as parents. Numerous excellent resources are available. If Common Core is implemented fully and not stopped, your children will suffer. True education is not what Common Core is about. As you have read, states are moving ahead with legislation to halt Common Core.

We have provided flyers, sample letters and talking points that you can use to talk with your local school board and principals. In our resource section, we have listed many references for you to further educate yourself with, as well as YouTube videos of lectures opposing Common Core.

One of the best overviews of Common Core is a YouTube video by Karen Bracken. In this video she tells us what parents are saying about Common Core and what their children are experiencing:

- Kansas children are required to wear "activity trackers," keep a diary of what they eat and are questioned in school about what they are being fed at home. Next year the meters will be fully implemented and according to the schools website, more intrusive measures will begin.

- Tennessee teachers are leaving the profession. One teacher takes a job at Starbucks and says the tradeoff was worth it. They are under extreme pressure and blamed if students do not perform to standard. They are broken-hearted.

- A Tennessee elementary school librarian shares that kids are bored with reading and losing interest. They want to read stories. Teachers are no longer allowed to bring their own creativity into the classroom.

- A Tennessee parent received a form letter asking her to allow her child to participate in a survey--TriPod Project. This is children evaluating their teachers' performance (funded by Bill Gates).

- A Tea Party leader obtained a set of principles that seem to support the idea of global citizenship.

Contact and Educate State Board of Education and Local Boards of Trustees

Attend local and state board meetings, and visit or call your state superintendent. These are questions you might ask:

- Where can I read our state's cost analysis for implementing Common Core and its tests in our state?

____

____

What will it cost us in our County?

____

____

- Where will that money come from?

____

____

- What is the amendment process for Common Core standards if we find out they are not working for us?

____

____

- Where can I see for myself the evidence that Common Core standards have been proven to be of superior quality and that they are internationally benchmarked?

- Where can I see for myself evidence that Common Core's transformations (deleting cursive, minimizing classic literature, moving away from traditional math, etc.) will benefit our children?

- The Constitution assigns education to the state, not to the federal government. Also, the federal General Educational Provisions Act (GEPA) states: "No provisions of an applicable program shall be construed to authorize any department agency, officer, or employee of the United States to exercise any direction, supervision, or control over the curriculum, program of instruction, administration, or personnel of any educational institution, school, or school system, or over the selection of library resources, textbooks, or other printed or published instructional materials by any educational institution or school system." In light of this, please explain why our state has agreed to intense micromanagement by the federal government under Common Core testing.

Talking Points for Letters

- We are tired of being told that these standards are state-led initiative. Teachers, administrators, professionals may have been working on standards for years but they clearly were not the Common Core Standards.

- The educational establishment has been educated about Common Core by groups and individuals such as Pearson, Wireless Generation, Bill Gates, and others, who stand to make a lot of money implementing Common Core. Credible educators have published their assessments of the problems of Common Core. These are individuals who have dedicated their entire professional career to the education of our children.

- Where is the evidence that Common Core standards are not harming our students? Where is the empirical data upon which this transformative alteration will lead to a higher level education for our children?

- Can you point me to a study that shows that not teaching kids how to convert fractions to decimals is better college prep in the long run? Where is the study that shows that lessening the teaching of classic literature and narrative writing is going to benefit children as adults? Where is the proven, long-term study that shows that informational texts are more beneficial than classic literature?

- Where is the proof that the Common Core is academically legitimate? We know it was developed by non-educators: David Coleman, the NGA and CCSSO. We know it was most heavily funded and promoted by non-educators. We know it has been politically hijacked by the Dept. of Education and that Obama and Sec. Duncan claim to have given it to states (further crushing the claim that it was state-led). We have endless references for these things. Where is the proof that education is still locally controlled? There's a solid copyright on the Common Core. This is the opposite of local control.

- Common Core Standards, tests and data collecting tentacles will strangle freedom and creativity in the educational system. The people who will suffer most are the children and the teachers.

Start an Email Campaign

Meet with your representatives in congress, the local school board of trustees, superintendent, and curriculum director. Express your concerns about Common Core and if you are able give them this book. Start an email campaign. Join together with others of like mind and coordinate an email campaign where selected articles on a weekly basis are sent further educating those in decision making positions. Every week they would receive several articles from different people.

This is how you might structure that campaign:

- Identify 8 willing people to join you in this endeavor. Even this small number will look like a great force because they will be hearing from different people every week. Each month the rotation would begin again.

- Select 16 articles for each month. You want well-written articles from different sources and emphasizing different parts of Common Core. Number these articles from 1 to 16.

- Divide the selected number of email recipients into 8 groups (number of people committed to doing it.) Number each group. Start out with each person not having more than 6 people to send a letter or email to each time. Recipients for these mailings would be those in the legislature, state board of education, superintendent, local school boards and anyone else that you think could be influential in defeating Common Core.

- On Monday and Thursday of each week send an article to your assigned group. Half of the people would send article no. 1 on Monday and half of the people would send article no. 2. Switch those around for Thursday. We don't want the board of trustees all getting the same article. They might compare notes and realize they were all coming from one source even though they came from different people.

- Continue on the next week using the same pattern but advancing to article no. 3 and 4.

- In effect, your selected email or mail recipients will be receiving two emails or copies of articles in the mail (which ever you choose to do) every week but they will be from different people.

This will keep Common Core in front of them all the time. The next month meet again with everyone bringing 3 or 4 of their favorite articles that they want to share and the group can decide on 16 of them. You only have to meet once a month and spend maximum of 1 hour a week (1/2 hour on 2 different days) emailing or sending in mail the group you are responsible for. If sending by mail, we would personalize by underlining something or making some comments. Always add a little personal note be it an email or an actual article you send. As you are able to handle the number of people in the groups add more. If you decided to send articles in the mail you could get them all ready to go at one time and just mail them at appropriate times.

Here are some suggested articles:

- “Classroom chaos? Critics blast new Common Core education standards" at FoxNews.com.

- "Clash over Common Core: Opposition grows as national education standards approach" by Mike Jaccarino

- "Common Core Standards: Why States Are Now Saying, 'No, Thank You' by Suzi Parker

- "Common Core Math 'Experiment' in U.S. Schools" at Education Reporter

- "Common Core Standards Will Control You and Your Children" posted by Karen Schroeder

- "Education standards: Parents need to stop Common Core" by Kathryn Miller

- "Won't Get Fooled Again? Reasons to Resist the Common Core" by Michael Paul Goldenberg

- "Petition to Governor Cuomo and the Legislature to End High Stakes Testing" by Carol Corbett Burris

- "Chicago History Teacher Calls for Investigation of Common Core Corruption" by Paul Horton

- "Common Core Harms Kids, Early Childhood Expert Says" by Nancy Nazworth
- "Common Core Standards for Public Schools: A Bad Idea" by Phyllis Schlafly
- "Pre-K Won't Help Kids" by Phyllis Schlafly
- "Principal: 'I was naïve about Common Core' by Valerie Strauss
- "Educational Accountability Red Flags" by Priscilla Shannonb Guierrez
- "Parents fight against high stakes tests and the common core" by Kristen Lavelle
- " McMillin Amendment Halts Common Core in Michigan" by Shane Vander Hart
- "Principal warns parents: 'Don't buy the bunk' about new Common Core tests" by Valerie Strauss
- "Common Core Standards Aren't Cheap" in Education Reporter
- "Corporate Greed" Drives Union Betrayal On Common Core" by Karin Piper
- "Colorado School District Rejects Common Core National Standards" by Brittany Corona

There are hundreds of articles to glean from on the net. If the website doesn't give you an option of printing out the article, high light the article, copy it and then paste it into Microsoft Word or whatever word processing program you use. You can then delete out the extra things and have just what you want which is name of article, author and article itself.

Challenge to the Attorney General

The following is a document that could be used in addressing issues under the auspices of your Attorney General. Paul Horton, history teacher at the University of Chicago Laboratory School, through his organization Citizens Against Corporate Collusion in Education, demands the following:[81]

> As American parents, students, educators, and concerned citizens, we are united in opposition to the agenda of those corporate, foundations, and government interests that seek to influence local district boards of education, state boards of education, state governments, governors, and the Office of the lobbying and marketing at local, state, and federal levels. We strongly suspect the existence of quid pro quo understandings between the current Secretary of Education and Bill Gates, The Bill and Melina Gates Foundation, The College Board and David Coleman, The Educational Testing Service (ETS), and

Pearson Education LLC that amount to collusion between a Federal Public servant(s) and corporate interests that appear to be working together to limit competition in an open marketplace.

We therefore resolve:

1. That State Attorneys General investigate possible quid pro quo agreements between the above parties and members of state boards of education and commissioners.

2. That State Attorneys General investigate lobbying of the above parties to determine whether bribery laws have been violated

3. That all state governments conduct investigations of the contributions of Pearson LLC, The Bill and Melinda Gates Foundation, Bill Gates, the Walton Family Foundation, and the Students First Foundation to local school board elections and the elections or appointments of state education commissioners and state boards of education.

4. And that each state files a complaint with the Anti-Trust Division of the Department of Justice in Washington preliminary to discovery of evidence of possible collusion of the above parties.

5. We call for a Joint House-Senate Committee to be formed to investigate possible collusion and influence peddling between the above parties.

6. We call for the Attorney General of the United States to select an independent prosecutor to investigate the possibility of quid pro quo dealings and collusion between the parties above.

7. We understand that the Tunney Act does not apply to this case and we argue that is precisely why collusion is involved, to avoid merger or the appearance of merger that would trigger a court hearing.

8. We strongly recommend that the Special Prosecutor (6) investigate all contracts led by the Department of Education to Pearson Education LLC.

9. We strongly recommend that all State Attorneys General investigate all state contracts led by Pearson LLC.

This page left intentionally blank.

19 - People to Contact

State Board of Education

Fill in the blanks of the Superintendent and trustees

First Name:		First Name:	
Last Name:		Last Name:	
Address:		Address:	
City:		City:	
State:		State:	
Zip:		Zip:	
Phone:		Phone:	
Email:		Email:	

First Name:		First Name:	
Last Name:		Last Name:	
Address:		Address:	
City:		City:	
State:		State:	
Zip:		Zip:	
Phone:		Phone:	
Email:		Email:	
First Name:		First Name:	
Last Name:		Last Name:	
Address:		Address:	
City:		City:	
State:		State:	
Zip:		Zip:	
Phone:		Phone:	
Email:		Email:	
First Name:		First Name:	
Last Name:		Last Name:	
Address:		Address:	
City:		City:	
State:		State:	
Zip:		Zip:	
Phone:		Phone:	
Email:		Email:	

State Legislatures

Governor, Attorney General, Senators, Representatives - state and local

Governor and Attorney General

First Name:		First Name:	
Last Name:		Last Name:	
Address:		Address:	
City:		City:	
State:		State:	
Zip:		Zip:	
Phone:		Phone:	
Email:		Email:	

Senators - Upper House

First Name:		First Name:	
Last Name:		Last Name:	
Address:		Address:	
City:		City:	
State:		State:	
Zip:		Zip:	
Phone:		Phone:	
Email:		Email:	

Representative - Lower House

First Name:		First Name:	
Last Name:		Last Name:	
Address:		Address:	
City:		City:	
State:		State:	
Zip:		Zip:	
Phone:		Phone:	
Email:		Email:	

County Commissioners

First Name:		First Name:	
Last Name:		Last Name:	
Address:		Address:	
City:		City:	
State:		State:	
Zip:		Zip:	
Phone:		Phone:	
Email:		Email:	
First Name:		First Name:	
Last Name:		Last Name:	
Address:		Address:	
City:		City:	
State:		State:	
Zip:		Zip:	
Phone:		Phone:	
Email:		Email:	

First Name:		First Name:	
Last Name:		Last Name:	
Address:		Address:	
City:		City:	
State:		State:	
Zip:		Zip:	
Phone:		Phone:	
Email:		Email:	
First Name:		First Name:	
Last Name:		Last Name:	
Address:		Address:	
City:		City:	
State:		State:	
Zip:		Zip:	
Phone:		Phone:	
Email:		Email:	
First Name:		First Name:	
Last Name:		Last Name:	
Address:		Address:	
City:		City:	
State:		State:	
Zip:		Zip:	
Phone:		Phone:	
Email:		Email:	

City Government

City Manager or Mayor

First Name:		First Name:	
Last Name:		Last Name:	
Address:		Address:	
City:		City:	
State:		State:	
Zip:		Zip:	
Phone:		Phone:	
Email:		Email:	

City Commissioners

First Name:		First Name:	
Last Name:		Last Name:	
Address:		Address:	
City:		City:	
State:		State:	
Zip:		Zip:	
Phone:		Phone:	
Email:		Email:	

First Name:	
Last Name:	
Address:	
City:	
State:	
Zip:	
Phone:	
Email:	

First Name:	
Last Name:	
Address:	
City:	
State:	
Zip:	
Phone:	
Email:	

First Name:	
Last Name:	
Address:	
City:	
State:	
Zip:	
Phone:	
Email:	

First Name:	
Last Name:	
Address:	
City:	
State:	
Zip:	
Phone:	
Email:	

First Name:	
Last Name:	
Address:	
City:	
State:	
Zip:	
Phone:	
Email:	

First Name:	
Last Name:	
Address:	
City:	
State:	
Zip:	
Phone:	
Email:	

First Name:		First Name:	
Last Name:		Last Name:	
Address:		Address:	
City:		City:	
State:		State:	
Zip:		Zip:	
Phone:		Phone:	
Email:		Email:	

School District

Superintendent and Principal

First Name:		First Name:	
Last Name:		Last Name:	
Address:		Address:	
City:		City:	
State:		State:	
Zip:		Zip:	
Phone:		Phone:	
Email:		Email:	

Board Trustees

First Name:		First Name:	
Last Name:		Last Name:	
Address:		Address:	
City:		City:	
State:		State:	
Zip:		Zip:	
Phone:		Phone:	
Email:		Email:	

First Name:		First Name:	
Last Name:		Last Name:	
Address:		Address:	
City:		City:	
State:		State:	
Zip:		Zip:	
Phone:		Phone:	
Email:		Email:	

First Name:		First Name:	
Last Name:		Last Name:	
Address:		Address:	
City:		City:	
State:		State:	
Zip:		Zip:	
Phone:		Phone:	
Email:		Email:	
First Name:		First Name:	
Last Name:		Last Name:	
Address:		Address:	
City:		City:	
State:		State:	
Zip:		Zip:	
Phone:		Phone:	
Email:		Email:	

First Name:		First Name:	
Last Name:		Last Name:	
Address:		Address:	
City:		City:	
State:		State:	
Zip:		Zip:	
Phone:		Phone:	
Email:		Email:	

Religious Institutions

Church:		Church:	
First Name:		First Name:	
Last Name:		Last Name:	
Address:		Address:	
City:		City:	
State:		State:	
Zip:		Zip:	
Phone:		Phone:	
Email:		Email:	
Church:		Church:	
First Name:		First Name:	
Last Name:		Last Name:	
Address:		Address:	
City:		City:	
State:		State:	
Zip:		Zip:	
Phone:		Phone:	
Email:		Email:	
Church:		Church:	
First Name:		First Name:	
Last Name:		Last Name:	
Address:		Address:	
City:		City:	
State:		State:	
Zip:		Zip:	
Phone:		Phone:	
Email:		Email:	

Church:		Church:	
First Name:		First Name:	
Last Name:		Last Name:	
Address:		Address:	
City:		City:	
State:		State:	
Zip:		Zip:	
Phone:		Phone:	
Email:		Email:	
Church:		Church:	
First Name:		First Name:	
Last Name:		Last Name:	
Address:		Address:	
City:		City:	
State:		State:	
Zip:		Zip:	
Phone:		Phone:	
Email:		Email:	
Church:		Church:	
First Name:		First Name:	
Last Name:		Last Name:	
Address:		Address:	
City:		City:	
State:		State:	
Zip:		Zip:	
Phone:		Phone:	
Email:		Email:	

This page left intentionally blank.

20 - Resources and Links

Websites

Danette Clark - - truly an investigative journalist that gets to the bottom of Common Core
http://danetteclark.wordpress.com/

Truth in American Education - a blog devoted to watchdogging Common Core across the country
http://truthinamericaneducation.com/

The MA-based Pioneer Institute - a think tank tracking and fighting Common Core
http://pioneerinstitute.org/

Hoosier Moms Say No to Common Core - ground zero for the parental revolt against Common Core in Indiana
http://hoosiersagainstcommoncore.com

Utah moms against Common Core have a great blog
http://www.utahnsagainstcommoncore.com/

Stanley Kurtz writes about Common Core at *National Review Online*
http://www.nationalreview.com/

Mary Grabar writes about Common Core and Team Chicago's lefties
http://www.marygrabar.com/

Phyllis Schlafly sounds the alarm on Common Core
http://www.phyllisschlafly.com/

James Shuls - A must read Common Core, math corruption, and need for school choice in *Education News*
http://www.educationnews.org/

Misadventures in the Common Core - A father's account of his 8-year-old daughter's math

homework
http://goo.gl/IpzBdq

My child's Common Core-aligned Algebra book
http://twitchy.com

Opposition to the Common Core Proliferating
http://truthinamericaneducation.com

Rotten to the Core Part1: Obama's War on Academic Standards
http://goo.gl/b7OJrB

Rotten to the Core Part 2: Readin'. writin' and deconstructism
http://goo.gl/is6VG4

Rotten to the Core, Part 3: Lessons from Texas and the Growing Grassroots Revolt
http://goo.gl/CjqA8Z

Rotten to the Core: Reader feedback from the frontlines
http://goo.gl/zRyCKn

Fuzzy math: A nationwide epidemic
http://goo.gl/AHXhvl

Everyday Math = junk
http://goo.gl/RUO17X

Obama's Sputter-nik moment: Cash for Education Clunkers
http://goo.gl/GWa87U

Barry Garelick - A New Kind of Problem: The Common Core Math Standards
http://goo.gl/roHgzl

Obama's national curriculum: Rotten to the Common Core (Part 1)
http://goo.gl/yo2yWU

The Dangers of Core Curriculum - In *Stand Up for the Truth*
http://goo.gl/lEM7ot

Reasons for Common Core Concern
http://goo.gl/dW0bBO

Common Core…aka: total BS
http://armyliving13.wordpress.com

Where Did Common Core Come From, Part 1
http://goo.gl/rNUc6d

Heritage Foundation Scholar Speaks Out on Common Core from Alabama
http://goo.gl/i3VJ5U

Is 'Common Core' Education or Indoctrination?
http://goo.gl/4hiY19

Children of indoctrination
http://goo.gl/KYidBT

3-year-olds chant "union power!" after reading new children's book
http://goo.gl/Maq5Ar

Attention, parents: Common Core opt-out form now available
http://goo.gl/oDF5cN

Indoctrination and Data Mining in Common Core: Here's Why America's Schools May Be in More Trouble Than You Think
http://goo.gl/j1Vsdu

Public silence in the face of Gates money kills democracy
http://goo.gl/6fNYNC

The truth about Common Core (Bill Ayers)
http://goo.gl/TcBWB2

Common Core standards will have feds forcing one-size-fits-all
http://goo.gl/jc5Hwo

Reorienting World Order Values Via the Intervention of Activist Education & Progressive Politics
http://goo.gl/ZAJ50r

Videos

Cato's Neal McCluckey dissects the Common Core folly
http://goo.gl/scqUsM

Pioneer Institute: Why Huck Finn Matters: Classic Literature in Schools
http://goo.gl/2dyjaQ

"Common Core Race to the Middle" Pioneer Institute
http://goo.gl/Z5B3uZ

Jamie Gass Common Core National Standards
http://goo.gl/QQS2EW

Homeschooling Advocate Warns Common Core Abandon Classics
interview of Will Estrada, the Director of Federal Relations Homeschool Legal Defense Association by Ginni Thomas of *The Daily Caller*
http://goo.gl/fWbUc6

"Reality Check: The Truth behind 'Common Core' " by Ben Swann
http://goo.gl/RjsSxV

Chicago History Teacher Paul Horton on Common Core and Corporate Collusion
http://goo.gl/8ZJk4r

Christopher Tienken - Professor at Seton Hall, NJ
http://vimeo.com/58461595

Jane Robbins – American Principles Project - Stop Common Core video series
http://goo.gl/9gN7ew

Senator William Ligon - Georgia legislator fighting Common Core
http://youtu.be/ODz4X0GO-Fk?t=1m37s

Senator Scott Schneider – Indiana legislator fighting Common Core
http://youtu.be/TH9ZxVrn6aA?t=1m10s

Dr. Bill Evers – Hoover Institute – Stanford University
http://youtu.be/LB014eno1aA

Robert Scott – Texas commissioner of education – rejected Common Core
http://youtu.be/WcpMIUWbgxY?t=2m25s

Diane Ravitch – liberal education analyst who just recently came out against Common Core
http://youtu.be/ZkZUGpJJWy4?t=13s

Dr. Sandra Stotsky, who served on the Common Core validation committee and refused to sign off on their adequacy
http://bcove.me/ws77it6d see min. 55:30

Ze'ev Wurman, math analyst
http://youtu.be/0cgnprQg_O0?t=22s

Heather Crossin – Indiana mother fighting Common Core
http://youtu.be/TH9ZxVrn6aA?t=54s

Utah moms Alisa Ellis and Renee Braddy
http://youtu.be/Mk0D16mNbp4

Jim Stergios - Pioneer Institute
http://bcove.me/ws77it6d

Jenni White – Oklahoma data collection expert
http://youtu.be/XTbMLjk-qRc and http://youtu.be/JM1CTJFUuzM

Susan Ohanian , education analyst
http://youtu.be/uJHkztNNFNk?t=23s

Dr. William Mathis of University of Colorado
http://youtu.be/46-M1hH0D1Q?t=23s

Seattle Teachers who boycotted Garfield High School standardized testing
http://youtu.be/N5ODEoqZZHs

Gary Thompson, clinical psychologist
http://goo.gl/rDYGNO

Emmett McGroarty, American Principles Project
http://youtu.be/wVI78lPCFfs?t=21s

David Cox, teacher
http://youtu.be/W-uAi1I_6Ds?t=22m28s

Paul Bogush, teacher
http://youtu.be/oaDniHquMVI?t=56s

Sherena Arrington, political analyst
http://youtu.be/QF337nKwx6M?t=6m35s

Walt Chappell, Kansas Board of Education
http://goo.gl/TQ45rp

Bob Shaeffer, Colorado Principal /Former Congressman
http://youtu.be/Fai4K2ZVauk?t=1m15s

Lindsey Burke, Heritage Foundation
http://youtu.be/1DOCH1YT6Uk

Oak Norton, Agency Based Education
http://goo.gl/KXhbDu

Chicago area teacher (Highland Park) resigns via this scathing YouTube viral video. Ten minutes long - worth the watch
http://goo.gl/fQCjPa

Education without representation, Karen Bracken
http://www.youtube.com/watch?v=0X0EFeH25bw

This page left intentionally blank.

21 - Two Sided Flyer Handout

For those of you that do not have computers, the next two pages can be photocopied as a two sided flyer. The next chapter, 22 - Our Online Resources, give links to download this and other flyers, brochures and handouts.

You might want to organize a group to go door to door and hand this out. Families with school age children would be the most concerned. Plan this flyer "blitz" a few days before the school board meets. You might also include a page with a Google Map of the location of the school board meeting. Include the actual address, time and date along with the map. When you knock on the doors and get to meet someone, urge them to attend.

Go to http://google.com and type in the address of the location of the school board meeting in the search box. Right click the map on the results screen and choose **Save Image As....** You could, of course, just print out multiple copies of the webpage. Here is a simple example:

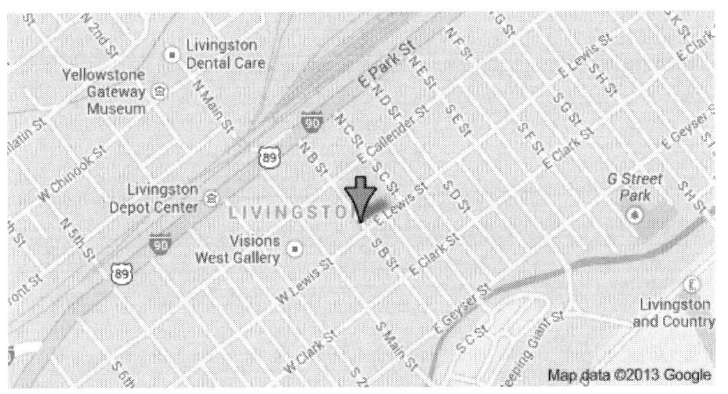

Help Us Stop Common Core
Join Us at 123 S B St to question school board members

The school board meets **Thursday, December 5th at 7:00 PM**

Call **406-555-9923** for details

ALERT! ALERT! ALERT!

Stop Common Core

Common Core Standards are to be implemented throughout schools across America in 2013/2014

What is Common Core? It is the stealthy federal takeover of school curriculum and standards across the country. The Common Core was developed without state legislative authority.

How did Common Core come about? Common Core was enabled by Obama's federal stimulus law and his Department of Education's "Race to the Top". The administration bribed cash-starved states into adopting unseen instructional standards as a condition for winning billions of dollars in grants. States signed on before the curriculum was fully written. Governors and State School Superintendents signed onto Common Core Standards without input from state legislatures, state school boards, parents or taxpayers.

What does this mean for the American educational system? American education will be controlled by a central authority. It will not matter what individual states, communities, schools, or teachers or what students wish to learn. All will be controlled and enforced by powerful bureaucrats.

Who pays for this new educational system? Common Core standards will cost states millions of dollars and this will fall on the backs of the taxpayers.

What is this "student data mining" all about? There will be a massive data tracking system on each child with over 400 points of information collected. The information can be shared among organizations and companies and parents don't have to be informed about what data is being collected. They will collect information such as: your child's academic records, health care history, disciplinary record, family income range, family voting status, and religious affiliation, to name a few. Your child will be watched from preschool till college (called Longitudinal Data System). You, the parent are unable to opt your child out of this tracking system.

Curriculum? Many believe the curriculum is mediocre at best. Basically students are taught to be global citizens rather than citizens with a proud heritage and individual, inalienable rights.

We all want the best for our children - come together, get educated and act on behalf of your children's future!

Myth vs. Fact

Myth Common Core (CC) was a state-led initiative.

Fact The CC standards were initiated by private interests in Washington, DC, without any representation from the states. Eventually the creators realized the need to present a façade of state involvement and therefore enlisted the National Governors Association (NGA) (a trade association that doesn't include all governors) and the Council of Chief State School Officers (CCSSO), another DC-based trade association.

Myth The federal government is not involved in the Common Core scheme.

Fact The US Department of Education (USED) was deeply involved in the meetings that led to creation of Common Core. Moreover, it has poured hundreds of millions of dollars into the two consortia that are creating the national tests that will align with CC.

Myth States that adopted CC did so voluntarily, without federal coercion.

Fact Most states that adopted CC did so to be eligible to compete for federal Race to the Top funding. Recession-racked states agreed to adopt the CC standards and the aligned national tests sight unseen.

Myth Under Common Core, the states will still control their standards.

Fact A state that adopts CC must accept the standards word for word. They may not change or delete anything.

Myth Common Core is only a set of standards, not curriculum; states will still control their curriculum.

Fact The point of standards is to drive curriculum. Ultimately, all the CC states will be teaching pretty much the same curriculum. In fact, the testing consortia being funded by USED admitted in their grant applications that they would use the money to develop curriculum models.

Myth Common Core standards are rigorous and will make our children "college-ready."

Fact Several states had standards superior to CC and that many states had standards at least as good. CC has been described as a "race to the middle".

Myth The Common Core standards are "internationally benchmarked."

Fact No information was presented to the Validation Committee to show how CC stacked up against standards of other high-achieving countries.

This page left intentionally blank.

22 - Our Online Resources

Flyers and Pamphlets For Your Use

We have collected and placed online some of the best flyers and pamphlets for you and your groups to use in their outreach and campaigns. Others created all of these and deserve the credit.

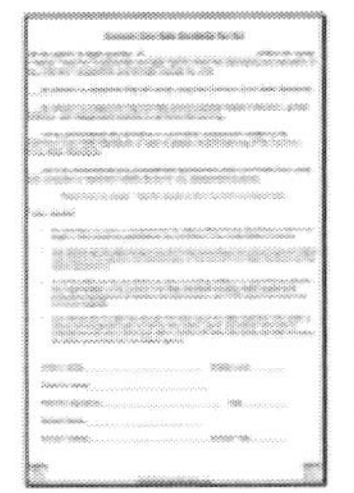

From the Truth In American Education comes this opt out form. Tell your school you do not want your children in Common core by using this Common Core State Standards Opt Out Form. You can download this from our resource page. http://goo.gl/P60Z4u.
8.5 x 11 - Black and White - 2 pages

ALERT, ALERT, ALERT (one side), **Myths Verses Facts** (other side) - copy on bright colored paper and use in your campaign to stop Common Core. Again, download our website at http://goo.gl/4whmwE.
8.5x11 - Color - 2 pages

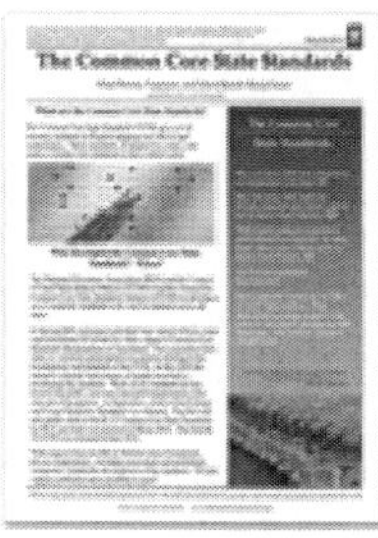

The Common Core State Standards is a flyer from Truth in American Education. It can be downloaded from http://goo.gl/JLnE76 and printed as you need for your campaign.
8.5 x 11 - Color - 4 pages
PowerPoint slide show for your presentations http://goo.gl/yzbtIr
8 Slides that match the flyer above

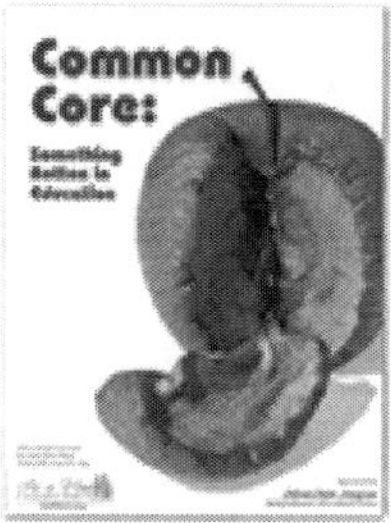

The Common Core: Something Rotten in Education flyer produced by A Sisterhood of Mommy Patriots can be downloaded at http://goo.gl/9kzcLd
Again, use in your campaign.
8.5 x 11 - Color - 8 pages

Controlling Education From the Top - Why Common Core is Bad for America is an excellent, detailed whitepaper written by Emmett McGroarty and Jane Robbins and produced by the Pioneer Institute and American Principles Project http://goo.gl/qIWNh8
8.5 x 11 - Color - 44 pages

National Cost of Aligning States and Localities to the Common Core Standards is another great whitepaper from the Pioneer Institute and American Principles Project. It was written by AccountabilityWorks http://goo.gl/kPj8tD
8.5 x 11 - Color - 4 pages

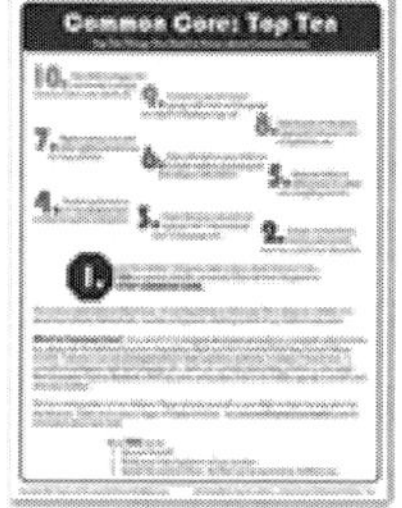

Common Core: Top Ten is another simple but great flyer. It counts down the top ten things we need to know about Common Core http://goo.gl/3Wm78O
8.5 x 11 - Black and White - 1 page

All Files in Zip

You can download all the above in a 12MB zip http://goo.gl/cavU3h

23 - Reach and Influence Thousands with Just MS Office

This chapter and the next are a little bit technical. Don't panic. We will walk you through the tools and processes step-by-step. There is a lot at stake and we are going to show you how to use simple automation to put a letter or email on the doorstep, so to speak, on everyone that will decide if Common Core is good for you and your children.

How do you convince hundreds or even thousands of people that Common Core is a destructive force? You can use your computer and office automations software just like your representatives do when they want to convince you they are doing a great job in your state or national capital. Contact your representative and you will receive back an email or even a letter that is somewhat personalized. This chapter will show you, step-by-step, how to do the same. Imagine what a well-crafted letter to every decision maker in the chain of Common Core could do.

If you have a computer, you probably have some version of Microsoft's Office. While the illustrations in the book are of Office 2010, you probably can use this as a guide to doing the same mergers with any version of Office 2007 or newer, the newest being Office 2013 and the online Office 365.

The main purpose of this book is to help educate those new to Common Core about its potential to harm American education. If you are now convinced, this chapter will give you step-by-step instructions on using the automatic merge features in Office to send hundreds or even thousands of personalized letters and emails.

How to Make Your List in Excel

What's the Benefit?

Nothing influences our legislators and other decision makers like a personalized letter or email.

They know it takes time and energy to write letters and emails and it implies a strong commitment to the writer's point of view. However, technology you probably already have on your computers can help you send hundreds of effective letters or emails in just minutes. This chapter will show you how.

It All Starts with a List

Almost all Windows computers have some version of Microsoft Office. We will use these products in our instructions. Where there are non-Office alternates we will mention them, but Office makes the process much easier. This list file was created by Microsoft Office 2010.

We have provided a Microsoft Excel spreadsheet online that you can download. Download from **http://goo.gl/A0uWie**. If you're reading this from the paper version of this book, you will need to type the link exactly as you see it, including upper and lower case. If you are reading the eBook version, just click the link. Either way, you should see the download dialog. It varies from browser to browser, but here is what mine looks like in Foxfire. Make note of where you are saving. You will need to find and open the file once downloaded.

1- Download confirm window

Step 1 – Open the MergeList.xlsx file

By default and if you have Microsoft office this file should load in Microsoft Excel as a spreadsheet. However, you may want to save this to a folder so you can copy and reuse as you create different lists.

Once downloaded, find the file wherever you saved and double click to open. Initially, you will see that the first row that contains labels for the type of data you will type into the sheet. Do NOT change the names of these fields although you can add additional fields. These named fields will match the names we use in the letter, envelope and email templates you can download as the merge letter. After adding a few names it should look like this:

Position	Courtesy Title	LastsName	FirstName	StreetAddress	City	State	Zip	Phone	
Superintendent	Mr.	Baxter	Dave	1313 Lane Drive	Bozeman	MT	59715	406-223-1105	bbaxter@g
School Board	Mrs.	Cameron	Marian	504 N Main St	Helena	MT	59601	406-223-0090	marian.can
Principal	Ms	Durslin	Susan	134 2nd Street	Bozeman	MT	59771	406-220-5537	sam.dursli
Teacher	Mayor	Hendersen	Daniel					406-222-7777	

Missing address data means we cannot mail a postal letter

Missing email address means we cannot email

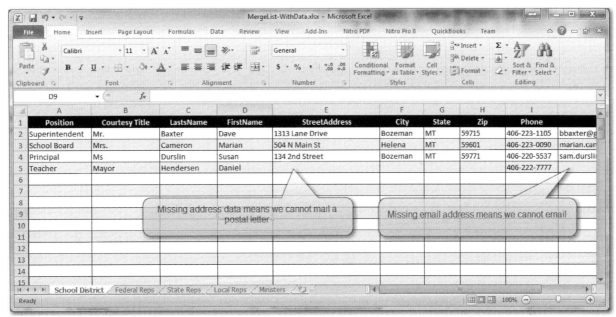

2 - Adding names, addresses, phone numbers and email addresses

Later, when you mail merge this information, this data will be inserted into the letter or email. Missing data can be a problem in that a mail merge will just show a blank. Try to get complete data if possible. If you use this list for an email blast, you must provide an email address. Do not use any commas in any of the data fields as explained below.

Notice that this spreadsheet actually contains several different spreadsheets. Excel calls this a book of one or more sheets. There are tabs at the bottom that differentiate the individual sheets.

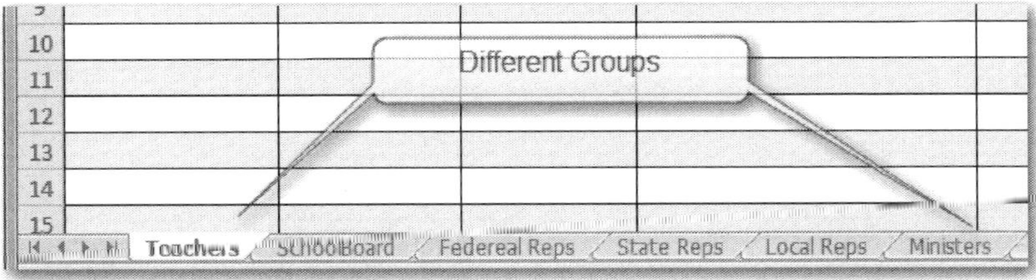

3 - Separate tabs for different groups

Step 2 – Saving the Data

You may want to keep the downloaded file blank. If so, before you add any names, click the **File** tab and choose **Save As**. Pick a location and give the file a new name such as "MergeListWorkingCopy.xlsx" as seen in Figure 4.

The next section describes how to find those decision maker's names and addresses.

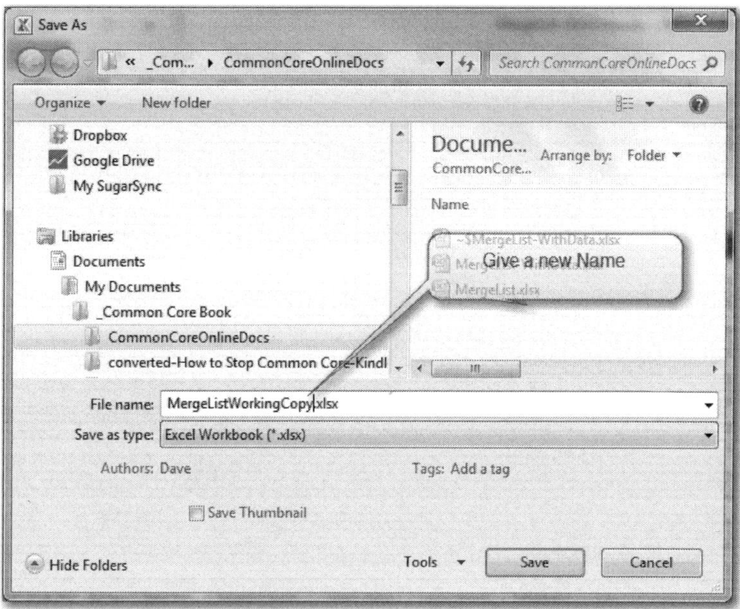

4 - Give a new name to the file

Where to Get Your Names, Addresses and Emails

You will need to use Google, Bing or Yahoo. In spite of Microsoft's Bing media blitz, we still prefer Google. We will also refer to a site dedicated to finding your representatives, state and federal.

Why are We Doing This?

To contact and thus influence the decision makers, we need their mailing address, email address and their phone number. In most cases, if they are important in the Common Core decision making process, they are somewhere online. The following show the techniques we would use in our location to glean their information. Your search will be somewhat different depending on where you live, what type of city government you have, school district, etc.

Finding my State Representatives

Step 1 - Go to http://votesmart.org/

Go to this website and type in your Zip Code; Zip+4 if you know it.

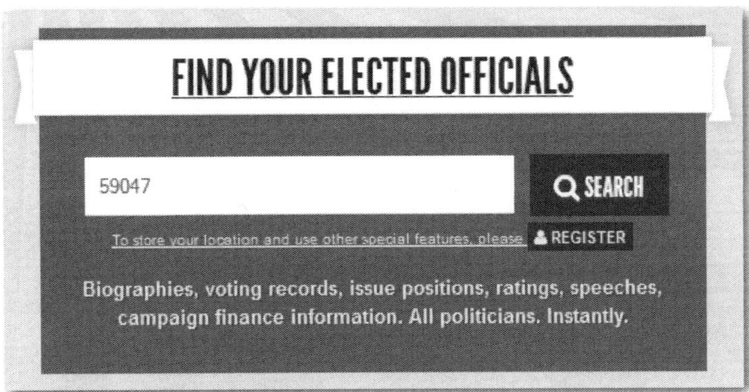

5 - Finding my elected Officials

Step 2 - Refine your Information

Many individual zip codes are split by one or more representatives. If you know your Zip+4, it will narrow the search. If not, you need to type in your complete address as you see in figure 6.

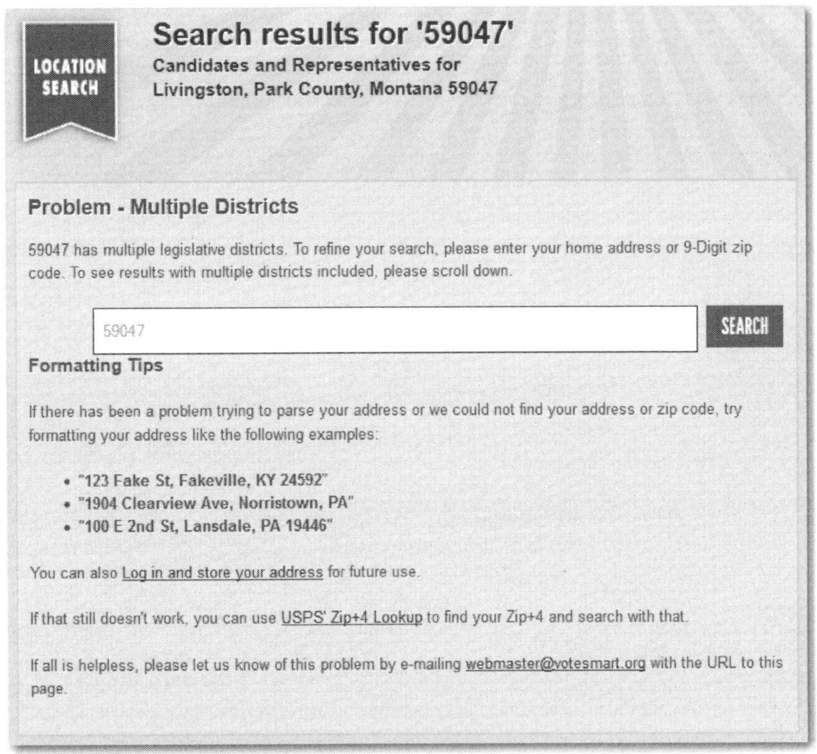

6 - Narrow the search by supplying more information.

Step 3 - All of My Elected Representatives in One Place

We have expanded out the section that shows our upper and lower houses of Montana's state legislature. Click the link to see Representative Neill's details.

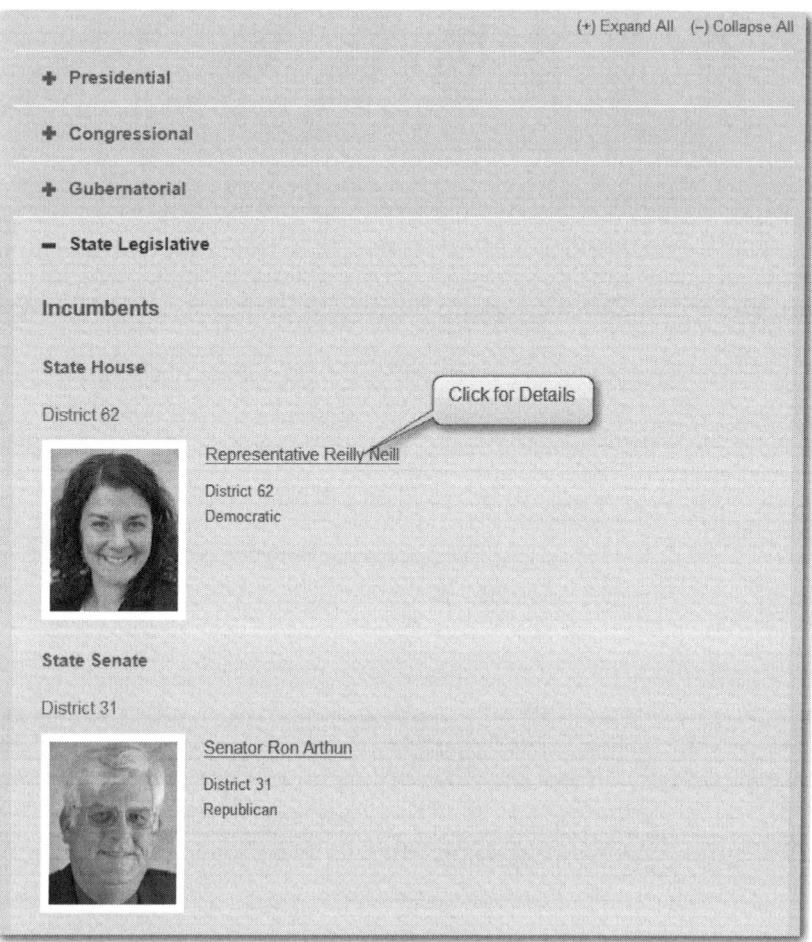

7 - My state legislators

Step 4 - Capture the details.

From the next web page, click the red starred link for contact information.

Here are mail and email addresses, phone and websites. You will record this in the spreadsheet we discuss in the next section, How to Make Your List in Excel.

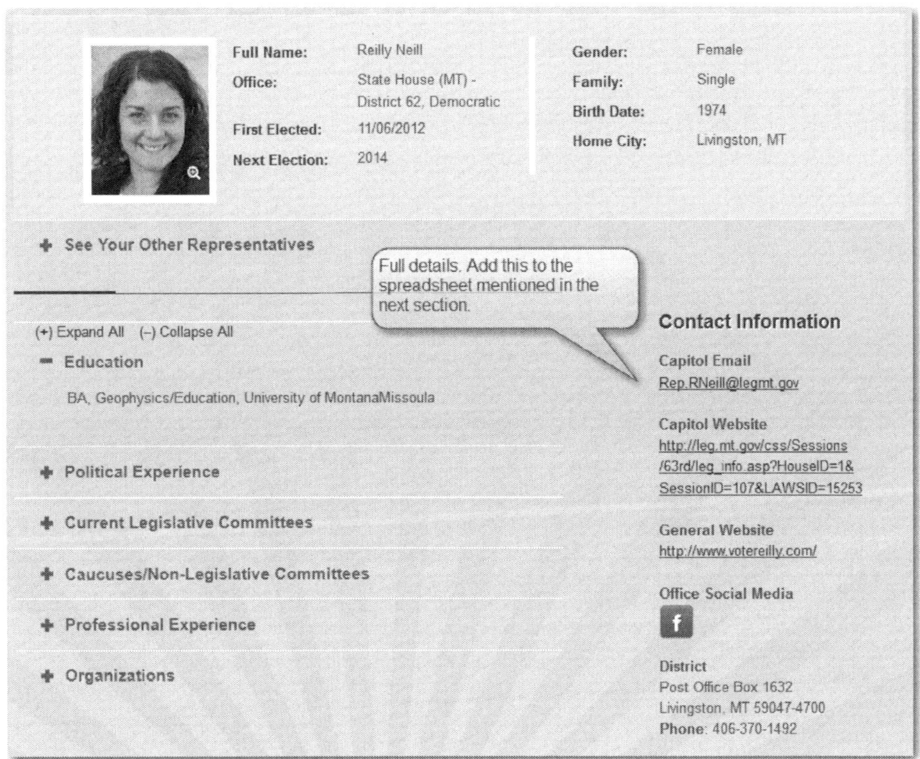

8 - All of the representative's details

Step 5 - Get the Rest of Your Representatives Information

Take your time and explore. From the President and his cabinet to your local county commissioners, you can collect the information you need to contact them as you will see later.

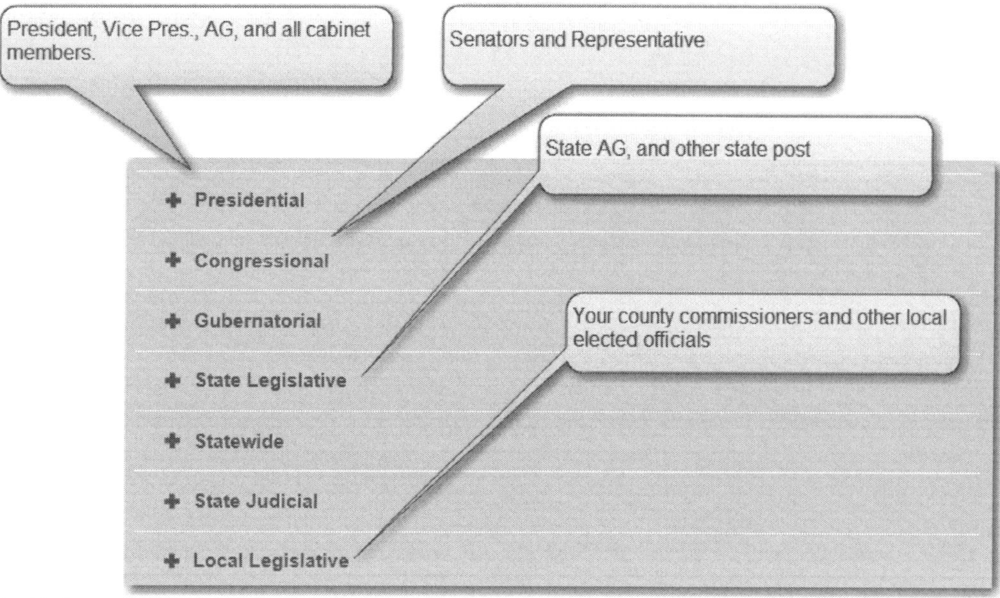

9 - All of your government is here

Finding Your Local City and School Officials

Step 1 - Finding City Officials

Using Google, search for something like; <your city> <your state> City Officials. When we did, we found two entries.

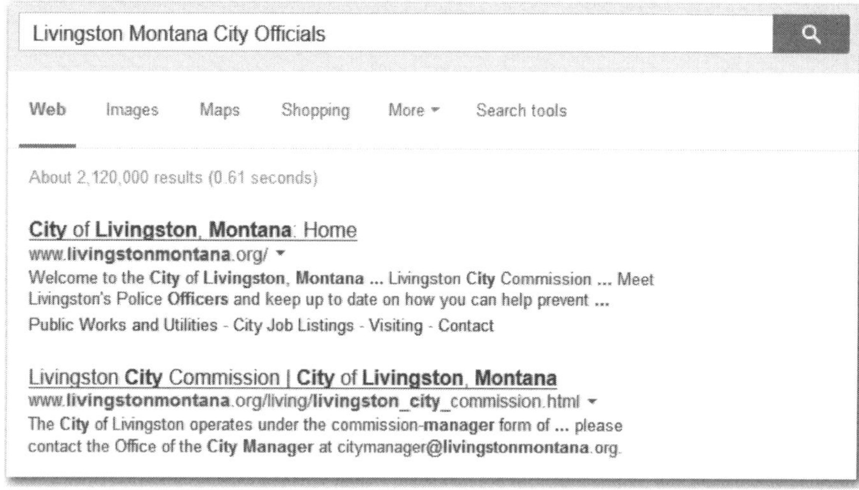

10 - Finding contact info on city officials

Step 2 - Drill Down to Details

The second Google Link takes us to the city commission's webpage. Each commissioner has an email link on their bio page. No phone numbers or addresses, but a call to the city offices can provide or forward mail.

11 - All 5 commissioners with links to their info

Another search gave us the city manager.

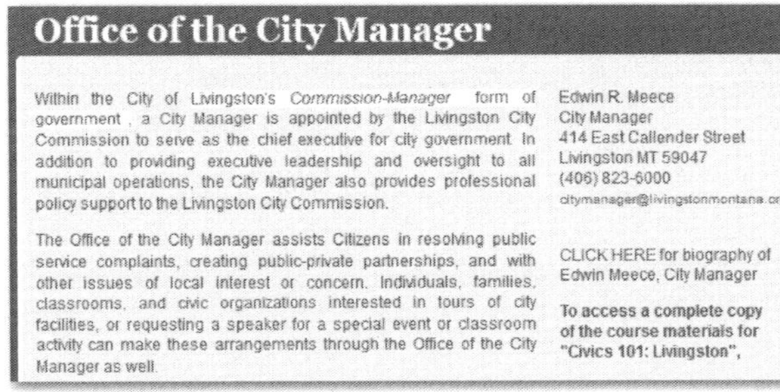

12 - City manager's information

Finding your School Board Members

we did a Google search on “Livingston Montana school board”. We got several results and explored them. After a few clicks, we found the official Livingston Public Schools website and it linked to the school board page seen below in figure 13.

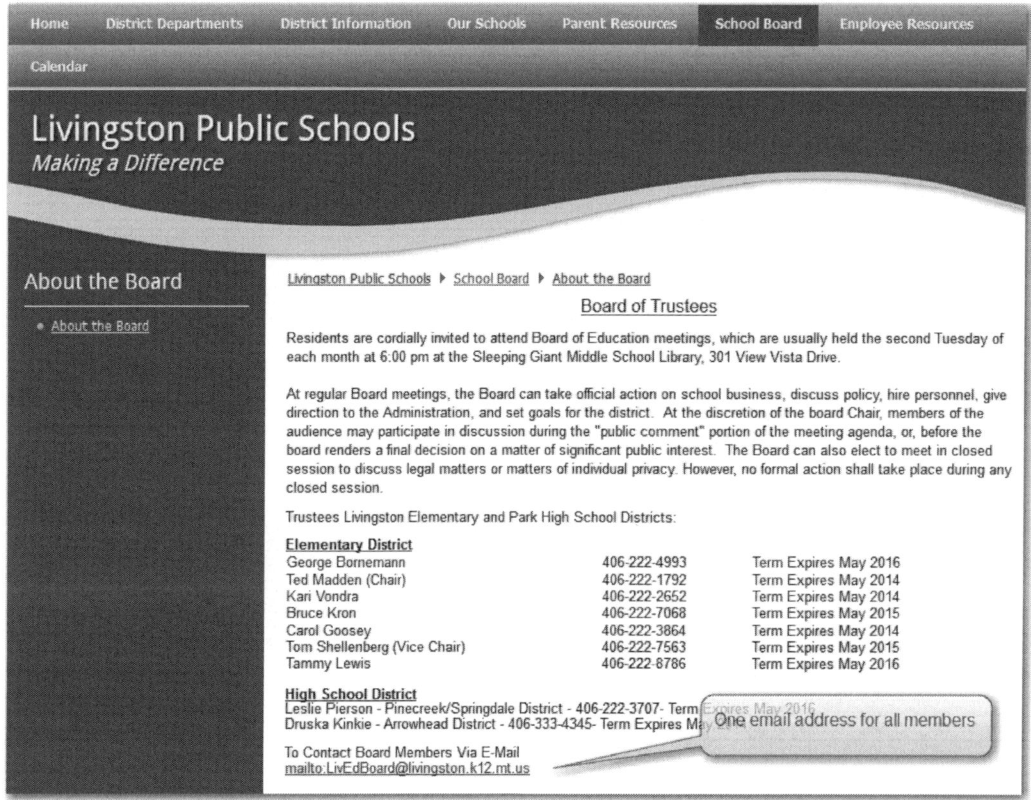

13 - List of local school board members

There are no individual email or postal addresses. This is common for local officials. You could send individual letters to the school district office. They do have phone numbers and a call might get you additional information.

If you are organizing a campaign with other “no Common Core” advocates, it would be worthwhile to contact them for individual information.

What is the Best Way to Contact?

There are several ways of contacting the person you wish to influence. In order of how great they influence or effect the recipient, they are:

1. Send them a personalized letter. By adding their name, or personalizing, the letter implies you took the time to write the letter just to them, bought a stamp and made a trip to the post office.

2. Call them on the phone. This cannot be automated, but a phone conversation can have a huge impact if done right. You should have a script so you stay on point and don't digress or ramble. Here are some do's and do not's:

    a. Your mission is to convince and convert, not browbeat. While you may have strong and perhaps negative feelings, being nice will give you better success.

    b. Don't threaten. You may/should know a lot more about Common Core than them. Start by asking them what they know.

    c. Ask if you can send them some information, as an educational expert, to evaluate. This may help get their addresses and, of course, follow up.

    d. Practice with someone over a phone. Have your phone partner play the part of antagonist so you will know how to handle pushback later. Practice until you are very comfortable discussing Common Core. Have facts and comments of well-known education leaders at hand to quote.

3. Email them. This is the least effective as most of us get so much email that much gets lost. This is particularly true of text based email. A good, colorful and professional email message is more effective, but is beyond the scope of most nontechnical people.

    If you do email them, try to personalize the email to use their first name. We will learn how to do that later in the section **Creating and Sending Personalized Emails Using Outlook.**

Creating and Merging Letters and Emails

When you want to send personalized letters or emails to recipients in your address list, you can use mail merge to create them. Each message has the same kind of static information, yet some of the content of each message is unique. For example, in your emails or letters, each message can be personalized to address each person by name. The unique information in each message comes from entries in the Excel file we discussed back in the section, **How to Make Your List in Excel**.

Let's walk you through the process step-by-step.

Step 1 - Set Up Your Letter or E mail Message

From now on we are just going to use the term **message** for both letters and emails as the process is similar. We are going to create our message in Word and then send it to Outlook to broadcast email or print as letters. Start Microsoft Word into a blank document. Leave it open as you perform the next few steps. On the mailings tab, in the **Start Mail Merge** group, click **Email**

Messages or **Letters** if you wish to print. Notice you can also choose **Envelopes…** and **Labels…**

We will not cover how to merge envelopes and labels in this book, but once you have done letters, you should be able to follow the similar steps.

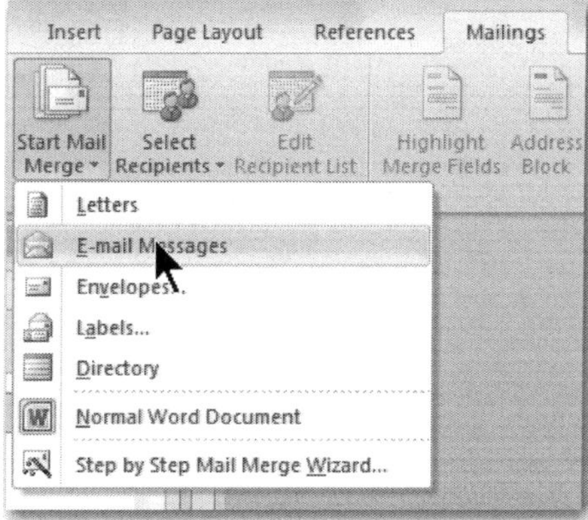

14 - Setting up the message document

While most of the following images pertain to creating merged emails, the steps for letters are almost identical until the very end. At the end of the process you would choose letters rather than email.

If you need to stop working on a mail merge, you can save the email message main document and resume the merge later. Word retains the data source and field information. If you were using the Mail Merge task pane, Word returns to your place in the task pane when you resume the merge.

Step 2 - Connect Your Message to Your Address List

To merge information into your message main document, you must connect the document to your address list. You created this list in the Excel spreadsheet in the previous section, **How to Make Your List in Excel**.

Since you already have a Microsoft Office Excel worksheet, click **Use Existing List**, and then locate the file in the **Select Data Source** dialog box.

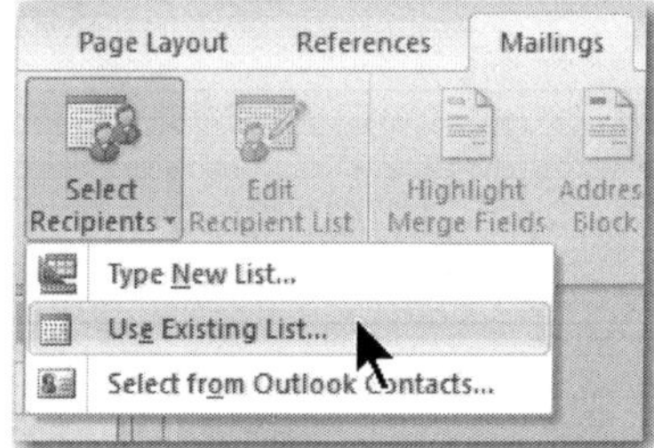

15 - You want to pick the list you created

You will need to remember where you saved the Excel MergeList.xlsx file containing your names and email addresses. Find it, click on it and click the Open button.

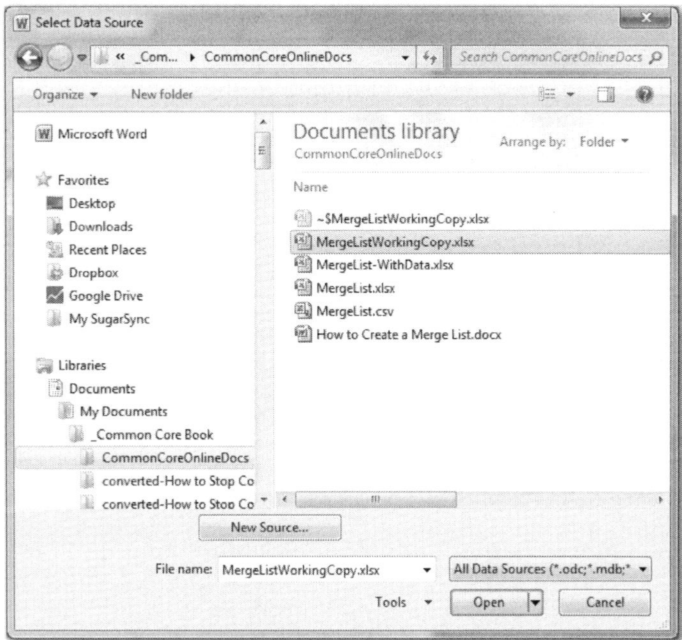

16 - Pick your Excel spreadsheet list

Since an Excel spreadsheet can contain multiple books, you need to tell Word which sheet you wish to use. For our example, we saw data in the School District tab.

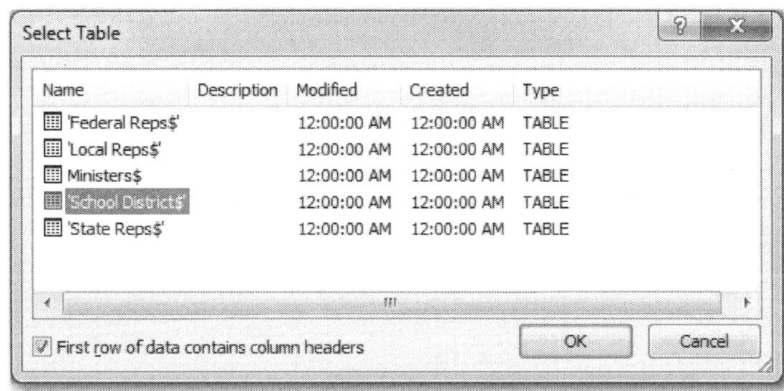

17 - Pick the sheet (table) that contains your records

Step 3 - Adjust Your List of Recipients

On the **Mailings** tab, in the **Start Mail Merge** group, click **Edit Recipient List.** In the Mail Merge Recipients dialog box in the Mail Merge Recipients dialog box, do any of the following:

Select individual records. By default, all records are selected. Click the top check mark to deselect everyone. Note that you can select or deselect all as a starting point.

Unfortunately, the merge tool thinks we want to send everyone, including blank rows, an email. We need to first deselect all rows and then reselect just the ones we want to send. Make sure to not select any rows that do not have email addresses.

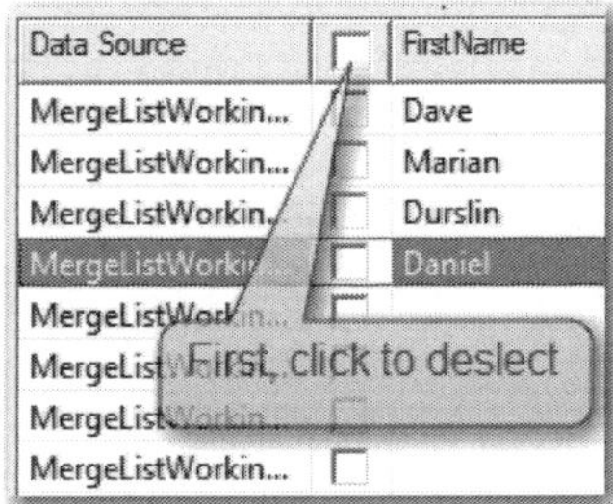

18 - First, deselect all

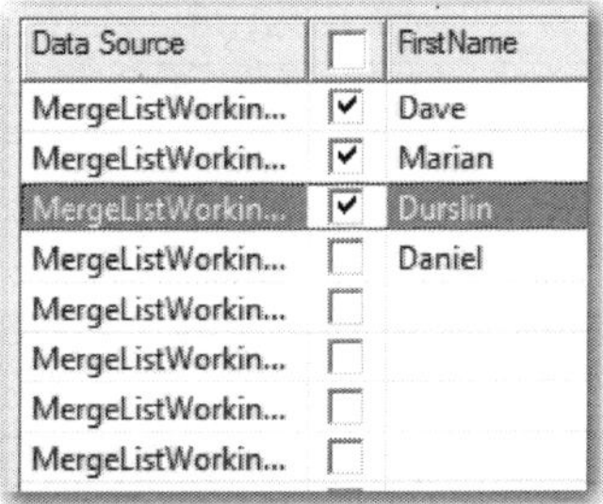

19 - Then select just the ones to include

Sort records. While this makes little sense on email, you could have them merged in a sorted order. However, if you were printing a lot of letters sorting is essential. You would then match the sort order when you were printing the matching envelopes or labels.

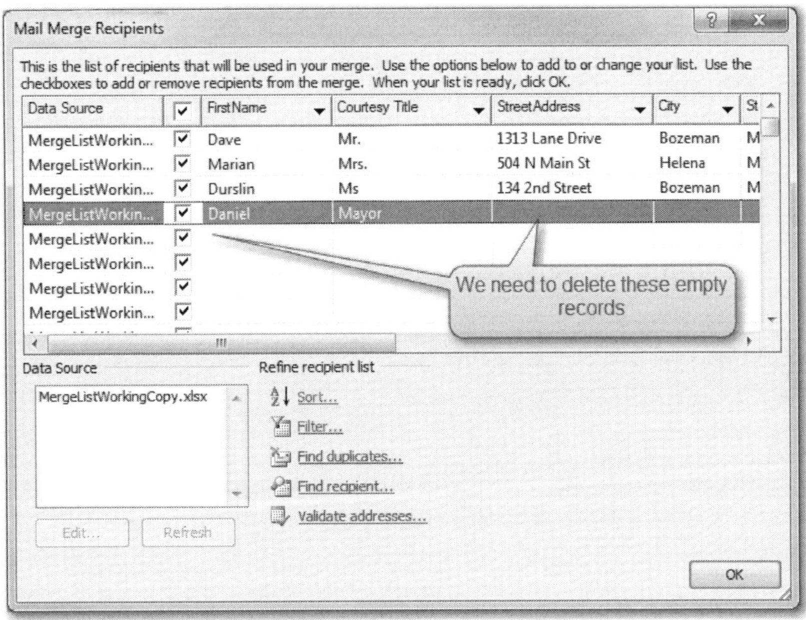

20 - Pick Recipients, Sort and Filter

Filter records. If you wanted to send the message only to teachers, you might filter the records by saying **Position** is **Equal to Teachers**.

21 - Filter dialog

Step 4 - Add Merge Fields to Your Message

After you connect your message main document to your address list, you are ready to type the text of the message and add placeholders that indicate where the unique information will appear in each message.

The placeholders, such as address and greeting, are called "mail merge" fields. Fields in Word correspond to the column headings in the data file that you select.

	A	B	C	D
1	Courtesy Title	LastsName	FirstName	StreetAddress
2	Mr.	Baxter	Dave	1313 Lane Drive
3	Mrs.	Cameron	Marian	504 N Main St
4	Ms	Susan	Dursl[illegible]	134 2nd Street
5	Mayor	Hendersen	Daniel	
6				
7				
8				
9				
10				

Category (LastName)

Records (Rows)

22 - Rows and columns

Columns in a data file represent categories of information. Fields that you add to the email message main document are placeholders for these categories.

Rows in a data file represent records of information. Word generates a message for each record when you perform a mail merge.

By putting a field in your message main document, you indicate that you want a certain category of information, such as name or address, to appear in that location.

Step 5 - Preview and Complete the Merge

When you merge, information from the first row in the data file replaces the fields in your email message main document to create the first email message. Information from the second row in the data file replaces the fields to create the second email message, and so on.

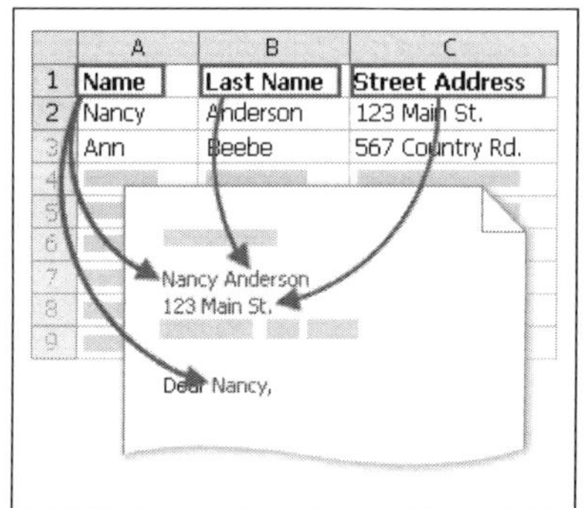

23 - Merge fields are filled from the spreadsheet

When you insert a mail merge field into the email message main document, the field name is always surrounded by chevrons (« »). These chevrons do not show up in the final email messages. They just help you distinguish the fields in the email message main document from regular text.

Place your cursor where you want to insert one of your fields and click the **Insert Merge Field** in the **Write & Insert Fields** group on the **Mailings** tab. This shows all of available fields. Select one and click the **Insert** button. we picked the Courtesy Title and LastName fields to use the person's name in a more formal way.

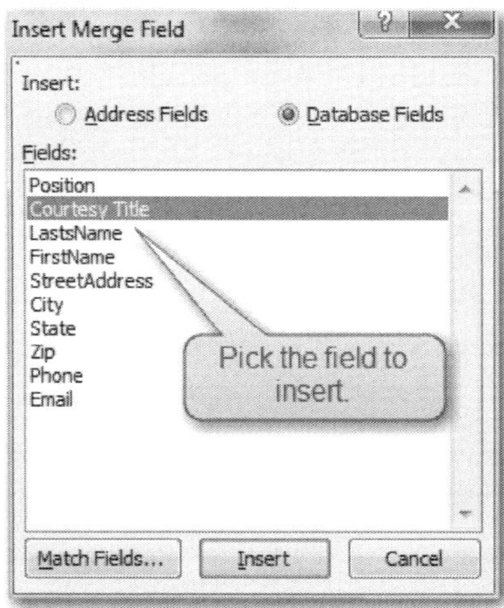

24 - Pick the fields to Insert

Here is what the message looks like so far. We have colored the inserted fields to make them more apparent. You would not normally do this as it would give away the fact that you used automation to send the email. We have choosen to use the more formal salutation "Mr. Jones" rather than the more familiar, "Dave". To do so, we must know the gender of the person's name and have that information in the Courtesy Title field.

Can you spare a few minutes to answer a few questions about Common Core, «Courtesy_Title» «LastsName»?

25 - Static text mixed with insert fields

Step 6 - Preview Your Results and do the Final Merge

To preview, click **Preview Results** in the **Preview Results** group of the **Mailings** tab.

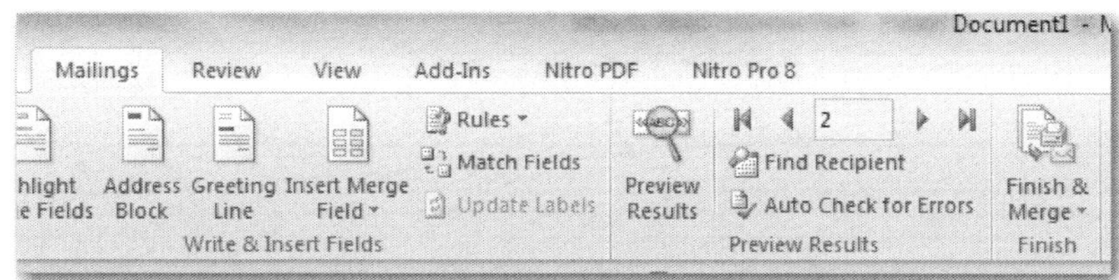

26 - Click Preview Results and then page through the emails

Use the arrow keys to page through the merged messages.

Can you spare a few minutes to answer a few questions about Common Core, Mr. Baxter?

Can you spare a few minutes to answer a few questions about Common Core, Mrs. Cameron?

Can you spare a few minutes to answer a few questions about Common Core, Ms Susan?

Before you do the final merge, you will want to finish the static content of the message. In other words, create the body of the email or letter. If you want to reuse this message in the future you will need to save it. Merging does not automatically save the master.

The figure below shows merging the emails, however, you could just as easily edit each document before printing. This puts all of the letters in a single Word file. You could then read and perhaps add more content to each letter before you print the lot.

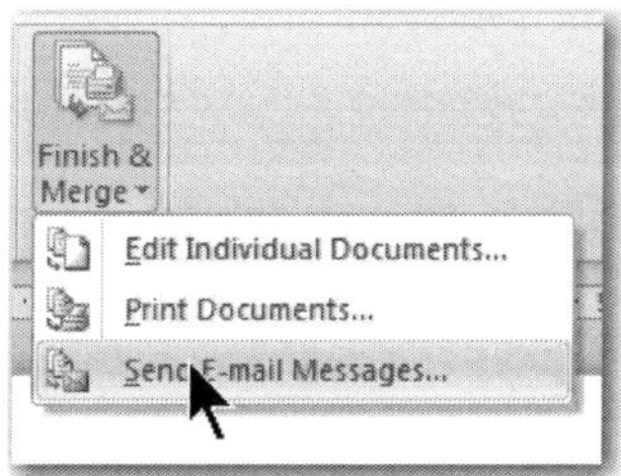

27 - Choose **Send Mail Messages...**

Finishing the Email Merge

This last dialog allows you to change the field that holds an email address. It correctly assumed that our field called Email actually held the email addresses. If it guesses wrong, you can pick the correct field.

You also have the opportunity to add a subject line. This should be short and should accurately reflect the theme of the email. Do not use a lot of unnecessary punctuation or all caps or your message will end up in a spam filter. My example subject line is "Could you help me understand Common Core?"

There are two kinds of email, text and HTML. The latter can have pictures, different size and formatted text and hyperlinks that the recipient can click to visit websites or videos you would want them to see. The best and default selection is HTML. When satisfied with your choices, click the OK button. Merging is very fast and you can see the field text changing in the document.

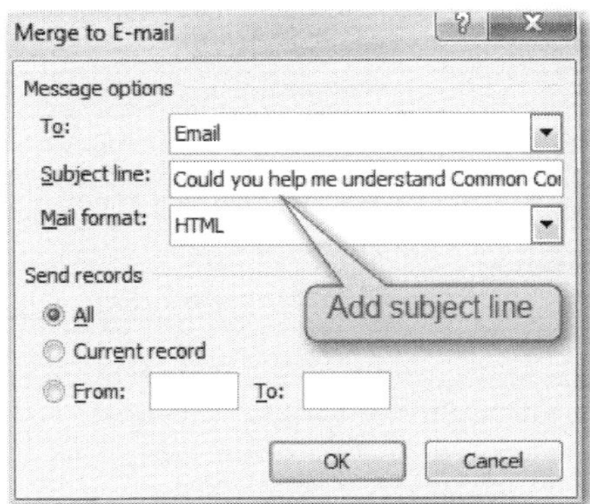

28 - Adding a subject line before sending

While nothing, other than the visually merging the document, seems to happen, the email have not been sent using outlook. Unlike the usual loading of a lot of emails into a single message, this type of merge creates a single email to each person on the list.

If you were to open Outlook and look at the sent folder, you would see something like this.

Date: Today

'marian.cameron@Yahoo.com'	Could you help me understand Common Core?	Thu 10/31/2013 1:41 PM	4 KB
'sam.durslin@msn.com'	Could you help me understand Common Core?	Thu 10/31/2013 1:41 PM	4 KB
'bbaxter@gmail.com'	Could you help me understand Common Core?	Thu 10/31/2013 1:41 PM	4 KB

29 - Sent email in Outlook

If you were to open one of the sent emails it would look like this. This sample is, of course, very simple with no meaningful content. Your completed emails would be much more complete.

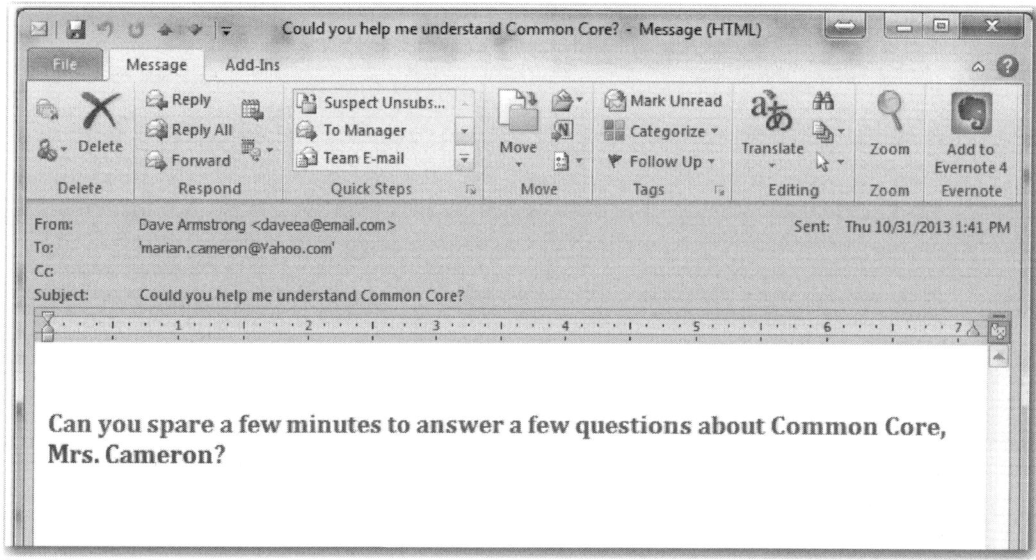

30 - A sample of a merged email.

Step 7 - Cleaning Your List

Emails may bounce or be rejected for various reasons. They might have a typo or may no longer be valid. About 20% of all email addresses are abandoned or closed down each year. You want to quickly remove these bounced email addresses from your list.

The bounce or error message varies, but generally looks something like this.

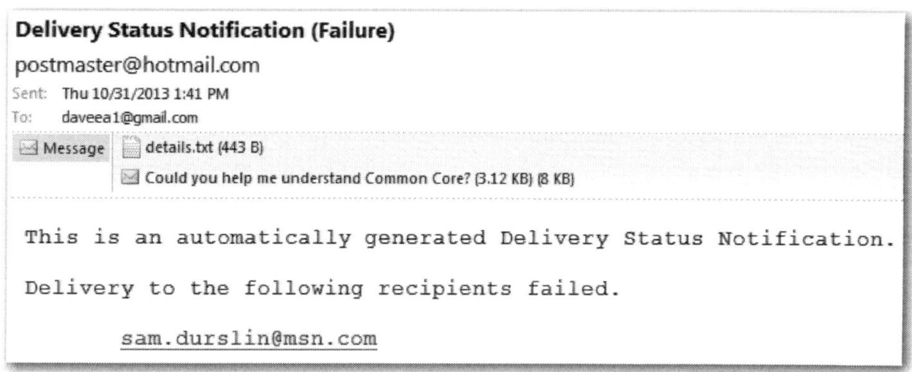

Delivery Status Notification (Failure)

postmaster@hotmail.com

Sent: Thu 10/31/2013 1:41 PM

To: daveea1@gmail.com

Message | details.txt (443 B) | Could you help me understand Common Core? (3.12 KB) (8 KB)

This is an automatically generated Delivery Status Notification.

Delivery to the following recipients failed.

sam.durslin@msn.com

31 - A returned no delivery email

Find the email in your list and click on the row containing the info. Then right click on the highlighted row and select Delete from the context menu. The bottom rows will move up and not leave a blank row which can cause problems when you reuse the list.

Finishing a Letter Merge

Merging to the printer is similar only you choose Print Documents from the Finish & Merge dropdown you saw in Figure 28. If you want to print a sample, choose **Current record**.

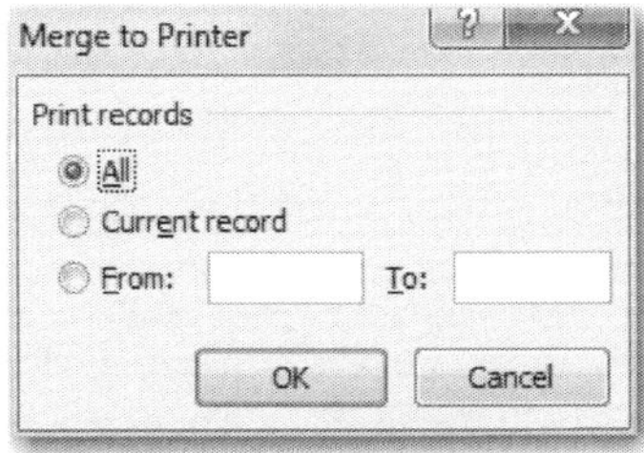

32 - Merge to printer dialog

Choosing **Edit Individual Documents...** opens a similar dialog that creates a new Word document that contains all of the letters which would allow you to edit each one before printing.

Careful with High Volumn Email Blast

Even though Outlook has no problem sending hundreds or even thousands of emails, your receiving email servers will. This email provider might be your internet service provider or someone else that handles your email connection to the web.

Your email provider is always on the lookout for spammers that would misuse their servers. They watch for emails that contain many recipiants in the To, CC or BCC addresses. Your Outlook merge makes a single email for each individual, but this may still trigger a negative reaction from them when they see a lot of emails crossing their servers in a very short period of time.

The key is to send only a hundred or so at a time and to spread them out over the day. If you remember, you can select or deselect individuals in the sort and filter dialog. You might deselect all of the names, sort and then manually select the first hundred and then merge. Make note of the ones you selected and then later, again deselect all and manually select the next batch.

If you have under a hundred names, you are always safe. Just, be careful with a large list.

This page left intentionally blank

24 - Reach and Influence Thousands with Just Gmail

The previous chapter used Microsoft Office to merge personalized letters and email. What if you do not have Office? We can do something similar using Gmail. This chapter will walk you through merging emails. While it is possible to produce printable merge letters, it is beyond the scope of this chapter because it requires programming or script generation.

Copying a Prepared Spreadsheet for Names and Email Addresses

Not everyone has Microsoft Office. You can still create a list using a free Google spreadsheet. To do so you will have to have a Google, and thus Gmail account. You only need to sign up once, it is free and it is easy. To sign up, go to google.com and create a new account. If you already have a Google account you need only to remember your Gmail address and password.

Here is what we will do in this section:

1. Go into Gmail and create a draft email with special placemark holder fields that when merged will have information specific to that recipiant; such as their name.

2. We will then use a Google docs spreadsheet which we will provide to hold the individuals to which you wish to send emails.

3. Lastly, we will merge and send a personalized email to each row in the spreadsheet. We will have a saved copy of the spreadsheet if we want to send a new group of emails later.

Before you can copy the spreadsheet, you must have a Google Account. If you're reading this in the paper edition you need to carefully type http://goo.gl/8cmYMO into your browser. If you are reading this as an eBook (Kindle, Nook, Sony reader or PDF) just cllick the URL link. Regardless, you should then see this:

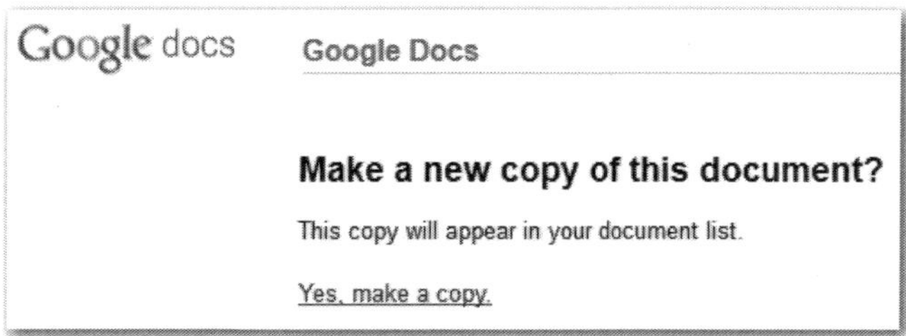

33 - Copying the custom spreadsheet into your Google docs

Click the **Yes, make a copy** link and a copy of the spreadsheet will appear in your Google docs. Don't worry if you have never seen or even know you have Google docs, you do and it is now open in your browser.

All Google accounts have access to the (free for individuals) office type suite within its Google Drive service. You get 15 GB of free storage along with applications that look and act like Word (documents), Excel (spreadsheets), PowerPoint (presentations), OneNote (form for collecting data) as well as a drawing program. You can organize your documents into folders.

This spreadsheet has custom automation that merges your data with an email. we have modified the fields to fit our task better, but the script and programming came from Amit Agarwal, a very talented individual. Type or click on this link to see his video if you want a more detailed explanation. http://goo.gl/sFHlo3.

Copy of Mail Merge Template

File Edit View Insert Format Data Tools Help Mail Merge Last edit was seconds ago

$ % 123 Courier New 11 B I S A

fx First Name

	A	B	C	D	E	F
1	First Name	Last Name	Email Address	Courtesy Title	Phone	Mail Merge Status
2						
3						
4						
5						

34 - Your copy of the custom spreadsheet

Now you need to start adding the information you have collected. The field headers are self-explanatory. It is important you do not delete any of the header fields in row 1. Start adding your info in row 2.

we will add just three rows to demo our example. Leave the **Mail Merge Status** field empty.

A	B	C	D	E	F
First Name	Last Name	Email Address	Courtesy Title	Phone	Mail Merge Status
Dave	Baxter	bbaxter@gmail.com	Mr.	406-223-1105	
Marian	Cameron	marian.cameron@Yahc	Mrs.	406-223-0090	
Susan	Durslin	sam.durslin@msn.com	Ms	406-220-5537	

35 - Add the information from your Google search

Creating Your Email Template

Most modern browsers have tabs. Open a new tab and go to your Gmail account. Click the compose button in the upper right. Do not fill in the To email section as the merge will do that.

Notice in the figure below that we have placed three placemarker fields that will be filed by the merge. Each starts with a dollar sign followed by a percent and the end of the field ends with another percent. The format is \$%Inserted Field%. This will tell the merge what field to match with when the merge occurs.

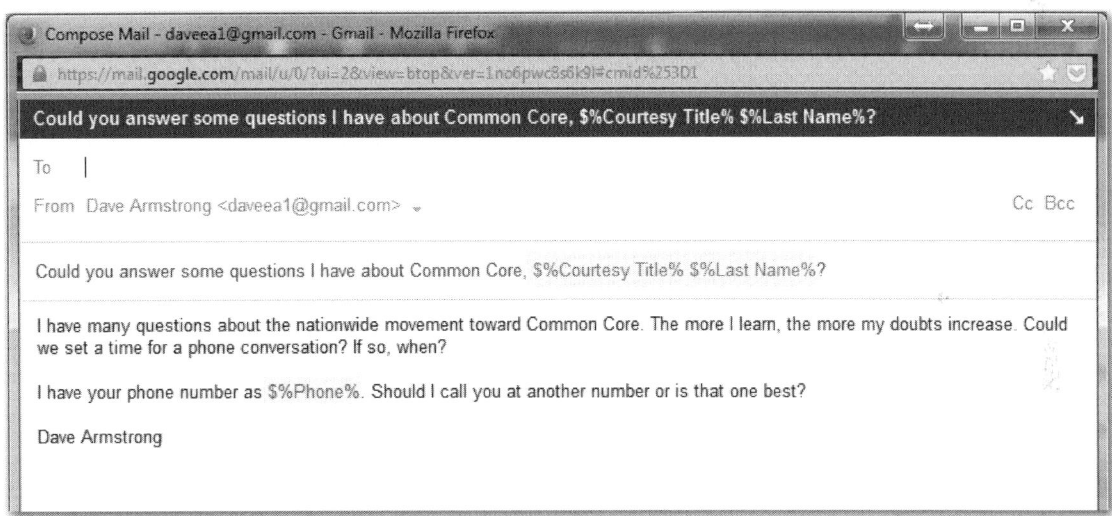

36 - A simple email with field place mark holders

Once you have the email setup, just close it. It will automatically save as a draft or template email.

Merging Your Email List

Return to your spreadsheet. If you left it open in one of your browser's tabs, just click the tab. Click the **Mail Merge** menu at the top and click Start **Mail Merge**. Careful you do not choose **Clear Canvas (Reset)** or you will remove your data.

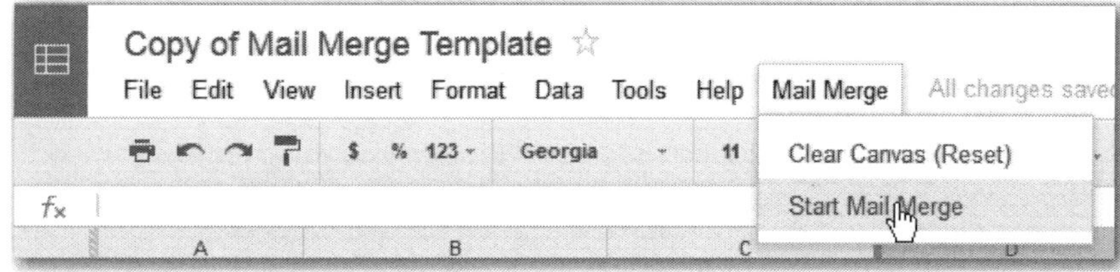

37 - Starting the Mail Merge process

The first time you run the mail merge you will have to authorize the process. On the first popup dialog, click **OK**.

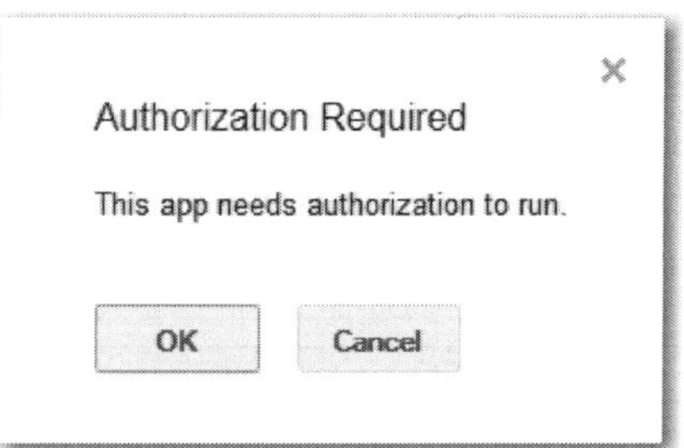

38 - Click OK to start the authorization process

Clicking OK opens another pop up screen warning you that this app, Google spreadsheet, wants to manage your email and run a script in the spreadsheet. Click **Accept**.

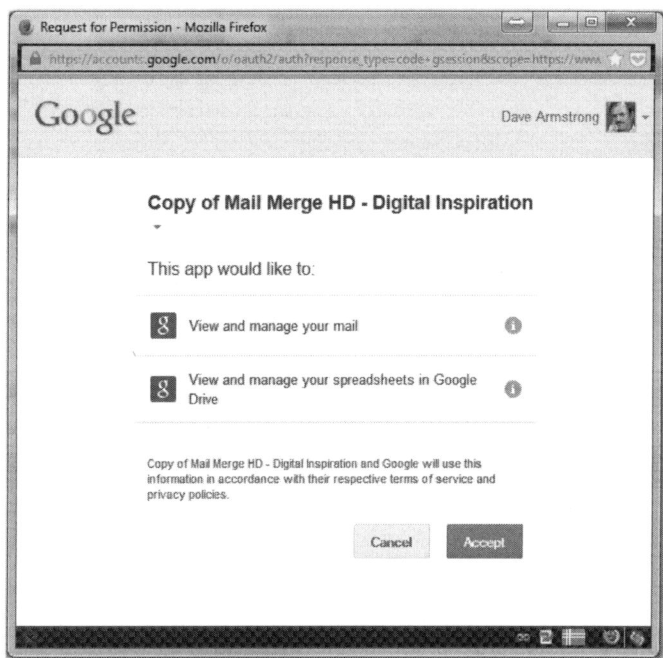

39 - This tells you what apps will be affected by the merge

This created no mail merge, it just told security it is OK to merge. You will now have to choose the menues **Mail Merge** and then **Start Mail Merge** again.

This opens the dialog you see in the figure below. Click the dropdown arrow and select the template we made earlier. You may have several if you have previous drafts.

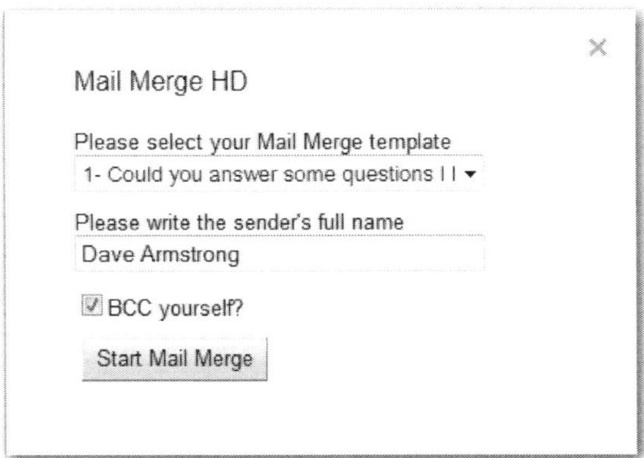

40 - Pick your template, add you name and BCC yourself

Add the name you wish to use as the From name and always send a **BCC** to yourself. None of your recipients will see your email address and you will get a completed email similar to the ones you have sent to the others.

You will briefly see a notification that the merge is running. After completion, a few seconds, you will notice that the **Mail Merge Status** column will now have **EMAIL_SENT** in each of the rows that were successfully merged.

Should you add new rows later and want to send just the new ones, this **EMAIL_SENT** flag will prevent the resending the email to them. Should you want to resend some or all emails, delete all of the **EMAIL_SENT** flags. Drag over them and hit the delete key.

First Name	Last Name	Email Address	Courtesy Tit	Phone	Mail Merge Status
Dave	Baxter	bbaxter@gmail.com	Mr.	406-223-1105	EMAIL_SENT
Marian	Cameron	marian.cameron@Yahc	Mrs.	406-223-0090	EMAIL_SENT
Susan	Durslin	sam.durslin@msn.com	Ms	406-220-5537	EMAIL_SENT

All sent

41 - Each row with EMAIL_SENT was successful

Checking Your Results

Returning to your Gmail, you should see your BCC copy of the email in your Inbox.

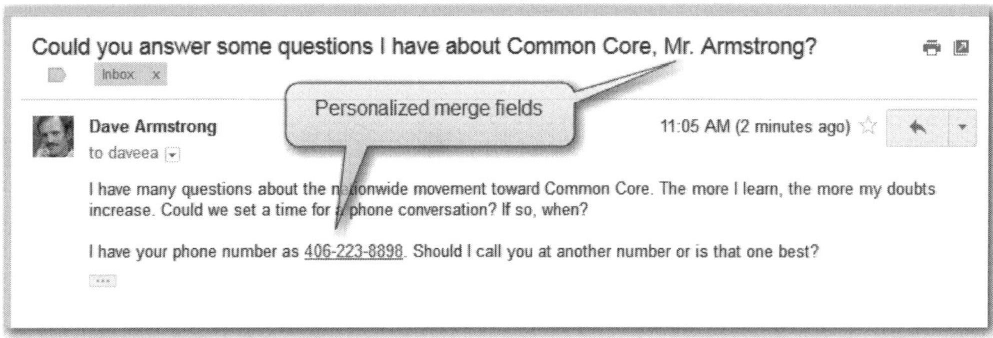

42 - Email with inserted merge data

You can look into your **Sent** folder to see all of the emails sent.

Getting Back to Your Email Template and Spreadsheet

The merge spreadsheet automatically saves, but at some point you will want to return to use it again. To do so, we need to find our draft/template if we need to edit it. If you go back to Gmail, click the **Drafts** folder on the left and you will see something like this. Click the subject line to reopen to edit if necessary.

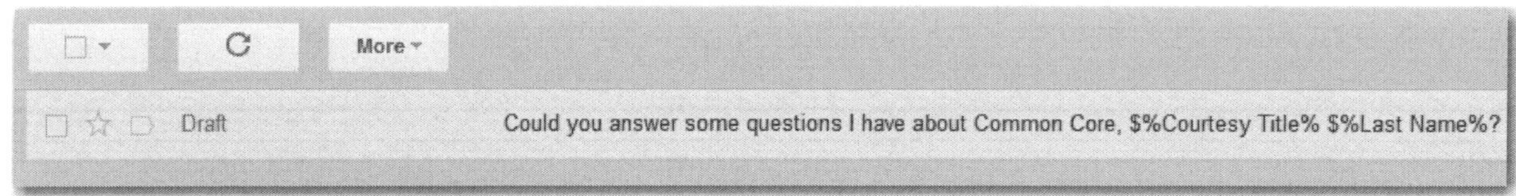

43 - You email template is in your **Draft** folder

To get back to your spreadsheet, go to http://docs.google.com and if necessary, sign in with your Gmail address and password. You may not have to sign in as Google stores your information in a cookie on your computer. Regardless, you will see something like this:

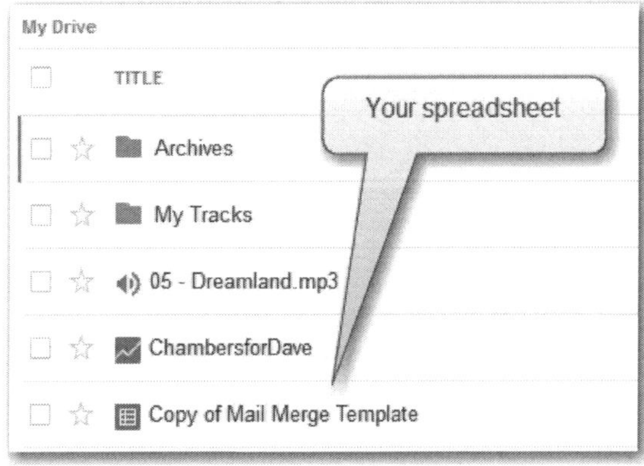

44 - Your list of documents and saved files

If you want to give the spreadsheet a more meaningful name, select it by clicking the small box to the left of the Copy of Mail Merge Template and the selecting **Rename…** from the dropdown **More** menu.

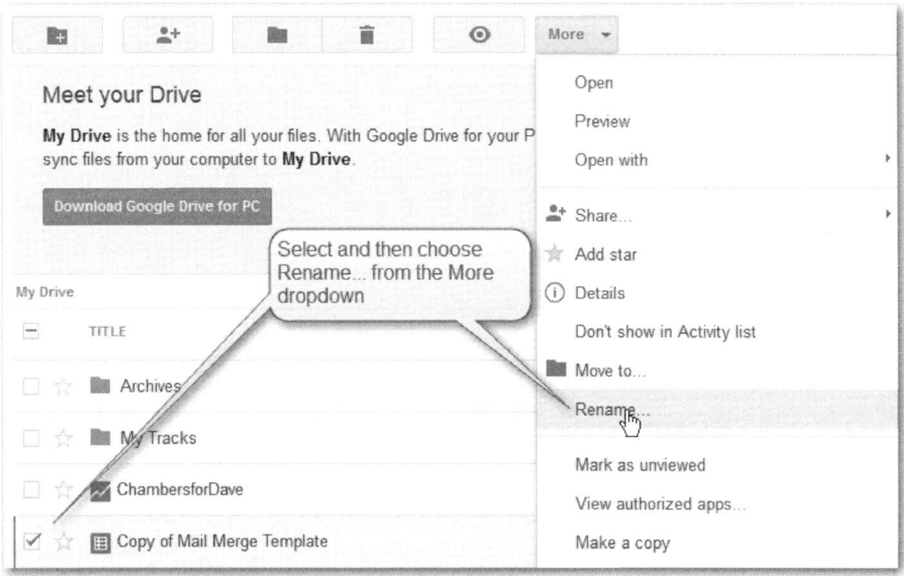

45 - Using the Rename feature

Type a meaningful name and click **OK**

Rename

Please enter a new name for the item:

School District

OK Cancel

46- Add a meaningful name

Warning, Gmail is Watching

Don't overdue the number of emails you send at one time. Google freaks when they see a lot of email going out in a short period of time. They will warn you not to use Gmail for SPAM. If you send more than 100 emails at a time they will warn you and if you send more than 500 emails within a 24 hour period they will lock you out of your account for a day. Keep it up and they will permanently ban you from Gmail.

Use common sense and spread them out over a few days if you have a lot of names.

This page left intentionally blank

Epilog

Does this book motivate you? Do you now feel committed to reversing the destruction and corruption of American Education? Great, we welcome you to the struggle. However, you and I cannot do it alone.

Share this book and/or ask others to purchase it and share with their circle. We have kept the price low as spreading the word is our real business. Selling this book is our means to that end.

You can purchase individual copies on Amazon. Should Amazon be out of stock, you can order directly from http://goo.gl/TVVi34. If you want to make a group purchase, contact us. Since we want as many reading this as possible, we provide group purchases at greatly reduced prices. Organize your group by providing each of them a copy.

Marian Armstrong
(406) 223-0090
marian_armstrong@email.com

ABOUT THE AUTHORS

Marian Armstrong is a former educator, courseware author, home schooler and researcher. She knows what makes a good education. After serious research, she discovered the harm that federal mandated standards, called Common Core, will do to our upcoming generations. She has led the fight in Montana to reverse the adoption of Common Core. Her latest book continues the good fight. You can contact Marian at marian_armstrong@email.com or 406-223-0090.

Dave Armstrong is a technology guru that has taught thousands of programmers new programming languages and software development methodologies. He is founder of Smarty Pants Social Marketing, a company that teaches small and medium size businesses how to master email and social media marketing. He is also the local expert of Constant Contact, the top email service provider. You can contact Dave at daveea@email.com or 406-223-8898.

Endnotes

[1] Myths vs. Facts - Common Core State Standards Initiative
http://goo.gl/2CYbXn

[2] NY should opt out of Common Core - Democrat and Chronicle.com
http://goo.gl/Dan2cB

[3] Two Moms vs. Common Core - National Review Online
http://goo.gl/jfSoT9

[4] School-Standards Pushback - The Wall Street Journal
http://goo.gl/xUGwf3

[5] Data Mining Students Through Common Core - The New American
http://goo.gl/U8YJz4

[6] Two Moms vs. Common Core - National Review Online
http://goo.gl/jfSoT9

[7] The Federal Takeover of Education - American Thinker
http://goo.gl/fJVJzU

[8] Don't Let Feds Control Local Education - The Heartland Institute
http://goo.gl/HUPfjI

[9] Montana State Superintendent Denise Juneau Explains Common Core and Responds to Opposition - newstalkkgvo.com
http://goo.gl/99YeDP

[10] Speaking Back to the Common Core - Heinemann.com
http://goo.gl/bhpGxD

[11] Why I Cannot Support the Common Core Standards - Diane Ravitch's blog
http://goo.gl/BBzJZU

[12] Common Core Curriculum: A Look Behind the Curtain of Hidden Language - CP Opinion
http://goo.gl/LgJtPQ

[13] Common Core: Phasing Western Culture Out of Education - Frontpage Mag
http://goo.gl/BRdXMb

[14] Common Core Curriculum: A Look Behind the Curtain of Hidden Language - CP Opinion
http://goo.gl/EUyVDA

[15] The Pedagogical Agenda of Common Core Math Standards - Education News
http://goo.gl/tFzjiU

[16] Common Core Curriculum: A Look Behind the Curtain of Hidden Language - CP Opinion
http://goo.gl/m62nw1

[17] Rotten to the Core (Part 2): Readin', Writin' and Deconstructionism - Michelle Malkin
http://goo.gl/CnW5w3

[18] Rotten to the Core (Part 2): Readin', Writin' and Deconstructionism - Michelle Malkin
http://goo.gl/CnW5w3

[19] Montana Uses Indoctrination Teaching Strategies and Adopts a Radical Resource Recently Banned from Arizona Schools - Danette Clark
http://goo.gl/17wP7M

[20] THE PEOPLE BEHIND THE LARGEST PROGRESSIVE INDOCTRINATION MOVEMENT IN THE U.S. - Danette Clark
http://goo.gl/Juuh0h

[21] Speaking Back to the Common Core - Heinemann.com (PDF)
http://goo.gl/Q8pk9L

[22] Time To Opt Out of Creepy Fed Ed Data-Mining Racket - Michelle Malkin
http://goo.gl/YyHudf

[23] Common Core as Trojan Horse - National Review Online
http://goo.gl/0z3JCf

[24] What 400 Data Points? - Truth in American Education
http://goo.gl/Vn1sWy

[25] The Sharing of Student Data Creates Concern in NYC - Conservative Teachers of America
http://goo.gl/5opbHZ

[26] Sample letter - State Longitudinal Data
http://goo.gl/5alCRK

[27] Written Testimony on the Common Core & Next Generation Sunshine State Standards - Truth in American Education
http://goo.gl/BXoN5q

[28] State Longitudinal Data: cuacc.org
http://goo.gl/EsR3IC

[29] State Longitudinal Data: cuacc.org
http://goo.gl/EsR3IC

[30] State Longitudinal Data: cuacc.org
http://goo.gl/EsR3IC

[31] Parents fight against high stakes tests and the common core - Bellmore Patch
http://goo.gl/KVumH7

[32] Petition to Governor Cuomo and the Legislature to End High Stakes Testing - Round the Inkwell
http://goo.gl/tiyhYW

[33] Massachusetts professors protest high-stakes standardized tests - The Washington Post
http://goo.gl/BVLG1Z

[34] Massachusetts professors protest high-stakes standardized tests - The Washington Post
http://goo.gl/BVLG1Z

[35] Time for Teacher Unions to Hop Off the Common Core Train - Education Week
http://goo.gl/FZuGh8

[36] What do you think of the Common Core? - The Classical Historian
http://goo.gl/5Qyr48

[37] Common Core: Nationalized State-Run Education - American Thinker
http://goo.gl/Owtg5s

[38] Love Child of Ohio Educrats and Big Biz…Common Core $tandards - Ohioans Against Common Core
http://goo.gl/2hZ013

[39] About-face: Montana to join Race to the Top, seek millions for schools - Bozeman Daily Chronicle
http://goo.gl/ta1RCx

[40] Is the Common Core a Runaway Train? Is it Unstoppable? - Living Behind the Gates
http://goo.gl/7lmeSd

[41] Report: Common Core Poses Legal Questions - Heartland
http://goo.gl/Gc3M88

[42] National Cost of Aligning States and Localities to the Common Core Standards - Pioneer Institute
http://goo.gl/vwNmaE

[43] Long Island schools opting out of Race to the Top - Newsday
http://goo.gl/F2U5J5

[44] Three Things to Simplify Your Fight Against Common Core - What Is Common Core Blog
http://goo.gl/WR1P8p

[45] Common Core Standards Aren't Cheap - Education Reporter
http://goo.gl/2boF70

[46] Arizonans Against Common Core Link Page
http://goo.gl/XroxM6

[47] Hogwash Alert: "National Review" on Common Core - What Is Common Core Blog
http://goo.gl/YY0Wq2

[48] Karen Bracken Speaks On Common Core At Tea Party Thursday - The Cattanoogan
http://goo.gl/S2E4PB

[49] AFT poll: Teachers unprepared for new standards - Linking and Thinking on Education - Joanne Jacobs
http://goo.gl/Vs4Jxb

[50] Turmoil swirling around Common Core education standards - The Washington Post
http://goo.gl/7sas7M

[51] Growing Concerns About Common Core Tests - WHAM 1180
http://goo.gl/lPbqek

[52] Union Leaders Love Common Core: Why? - @ The Chalk Face
http://goo.gl/UyiSj5

[53] School Choice? What's That? - Restore Oklahoma Public Education
http://goo.gl/wz8nnx

[54] Federal Title IX Enforcers Effectively Define Dating and Sex Education as "Sexual Harassment" - Education Watch International
http://goo.gl/pkDfp6

[55] Common Core: Nationalized State-Run Education - American Thinker
http://goo.gl/uDo6yc

[56] Public Invited to Comment on Common Core PARCC Assessment, But PARCC Assesses the Wrong Goals - The Report Card
http://goo.gl/fZx2Fp

[57] Look Who Funded and Developed Common Core - The Common Sense Show
http://goo.gl/vA8a91

[58] Common Core Standards Will Control You and Your Children - Political Outcast
http://goo.gl/rppkrV

[59] Governor Pence Pauses Indiana Common Core Standards - The Foundry - Heritage.org
http://goo.gl/ZoTlYm

[60] Texas Ends CSCOPE Curriculum System After Concerns That It Had An Anti-American Agenda - HUFF POST
http://goo.gl/b9Lupf

[61] Texas Ends CSCOPE Curriculum System After Concerns That It Had An Anti-American Agenda - Huffington Post
http://goo.gl/3llPyI

[62] Congress Tackles the Common Core National Standards and Databases - HSLDA
http://goo.gl/KUDt94

[63] Congress Tackles the Common Core National Standards and Databases - HSLDA
http://goo.gl/KUDt94

[64] Colorado School District Rejects Common Core National Standards - The Foundry
http://goo.gl/DQCB5C

[65] What Does It Take to Stop Common Core? Defund It. - Truth in American Education
http://goo.gl/TqUSci

[66] BAD ASS TEACHERS ASSOCIATION AND OTHER LEFTISTS JOIN FIGHT AGAINST COMMON CORE - Free Zone Media Center News
http://goo.gl/Vr57yf

[67] For Elected Officials who won't roll up their sleeves– "shame on them". - Mississippi PEP
http://goo.gl/b6UZqI

[68] CSCOPE Is Common Core & It Isn't Good - The Independent Sentinel
http://goo.gl/Hu4rGO

[69] CSCOPE Is Common Core & It Isn't Good - The Independent Sentinel
http://goo.gl/PN3SDt

[70] AGENDA 21: COMMON CORE IS INSTITUTIONALIZED TERRORISM - Democrats Against U.N. Agenda 21
http://goo.gl/QeT6FS

[71] Common Core Curriculum & Agenda 21 - Republic Magazine
http://goo.gl/L3OnLU

[72] Teacher's resignation letter: 'My profession … no longer exists' - The Washington Post
http://goo.gl/kk6XRS

[73] Fear and Loathing and the Common Core - Raging Horse Blog
http://goo.gl/jUC7vw

[74] A Wyoming School's Common Core Gag Order - Truth in American Education
http://goo.gl/fqCC7k

[75] A tough critique of Common Core on early childhood education - The Washington Post
http://goo.gl/mUqlYQ

[76] Principal: 'I was naïve about Common Core' - The Washington Post
http://goo.gl/p9YjsO

[77] This is an email I (Karen Bracken) received from a Mom - Tennessee Against Common Core
http://goo.gl/VqLFop

[78] Oklahoma Pastors' Letter Against Common Core - What is Common Core Blog
http://goo.gl/6sBh8h

[79] To My Students: 'I Love You and Believe in You'- @ The Chalk Face
http://goo.gl/pXBe1l

[80] PhD from Bulgaria warns us of things to come if we don't wake up many people. - Tennessee Against Common Core
http://goo.gl/Mu92dg

[81] Stop Common Core in Illinois Facebook page
http://goo.gl/Zshq6R

Made in the USA
San Bernardino, CA
19 January 2014